To Hippies, Bikers, and Punks with Love

by Dellana Zabel

Table of Contents

Acknowledgments

First edition published in Matthews, NC - 2009

Dellana Zabel

P.O. Box 552
Matthews, NC 28106
dellana@ashes-beauty.com

www.ashes-beauty.com
order@ashes-beauty.com

Printer: createspace.com

Book Cover Design and Sketches: William J. Zabel

Type Design and Publication:
Life Application Ministries Publication (LAMP)
www.lifeapplicationministries.org

Francine Blaine, Dellana Zabel, Gwen Bowen, Barbara Walker

I am eternally grateful to God for putting this book together. Thank you to my husband, Will, for the creative drawings and book cover. Thank you to Gwen for assisting me in the writing of the book.
Thank you to all my friends and prayer warriors who fervently prayed for the completion and success of this book, in particular Francine, Barbara, and Gwen.

Preface

This is a story about myself as near and as factual as I can remember. There are things I am going to say in this story that may shock you. But I want to share my life struggles and how the Lord has delivered me for the sole purpose of testifying to you that you may be set free too!

It is important that you know God loves YOU! The Lord did send His only Son so that you may have eternal life. I do not know of any person who would give their only son to deliver someone like me! God did. If you do not have an assurance in your heart of hearts that you will go to Heaven when you die, then you need to speak this prayer aloud:

"Dear Lord, I have made lots of mistakes in my lifetime, and I ask You to forgive me for each and every one of them. I ask that You come into my heart and be the Lord of my life. I long for a relationship with You. Lord, save me from the pit of hell. Thank You, Jesus, for dying for me and saving me. Amen."

Jesus can be your best friend. Please read about the life of Jesus in the Books of Matthew, Mark, Luke, and John in your Bible. Ask God to give you understanding with the help of the Holy Spirit.

I pray for the anointing of the Lord to be on this story so that you will experience the salvation and deliverance of the Lord our Savior.

-Chapter One-

In the Beginning

New life always begins when we meet the Lord and then decide to head in the direction that He leads. So I will begin my story setting the stage for when the Lord entered my life.

Bill (now Will) and I met in Helena, Montana when he was working with the Forest Service fire fighting. During that time, I had been working at the Social and Rehabilitation Services (S.R.S.) as a data entry operator. I liked my job, but I was basically a mess in every way. I would go to the bars with the girls from work to hunt for men. Searching for satisfaction in alcohol, I would end up coming home tanked and dissatisfied.

I went out one night by myself and ended up having a guy come home with me. He began to chase me all around the trailer wanting more from me than I was willing to give. The addition to the trailer had a door and screen door with two steps that led down to the ground, where I had a car parked beside the little truck I owned. When this guy was chasing me all around this house, I finally became very angry. To this day, I don't know how I did this, but I stopped by the door and opened it. When this guy approached me, I picked him up, opened the screen door, and threw him over the steps, over the car, where he landed between the car and the truck. I even followed him out the door, not even thinking about what I was going to do. The guy ran for his car and kept on going. I never heard from him again. I know now that God must have had his angels protecting me because this guy was much bigger and taller than me.

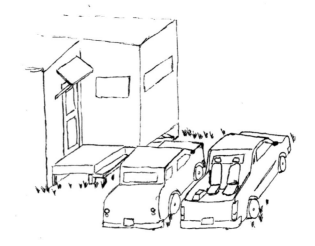

To Hippies, Bikers, and Punks With Love

The next day, as I sat out on the steps smoking a cigarette and shaking from the drinking, I screamed at the top of my lungs to God in prayer, or I guess that's what one would call it. I told God that I was never going to date or go to the bar again and that if He wanted me married, He would have to bring a man to my doorstep. Then I made a list of what I wanted in a man. I wanted someone the same height as me with blue eyes and a weight problem because I did not want anyone nagging me about my weight. I did not want someone who liked sports because I wanted him to pay attention to me completely. I also asked for someone with emotional problems because I pridefully thought that I was good at helping people with their problems. I also wanted someone loving, kind, and considerate. Now I have since repented to the Lord for those stupid requests. Always be mindful of what you pray for, you will sometimes get it and I did.

After I had made my list, prayed over it, and finished screaming at God, I did not go out much at all except with my friends to their homes. When I did venture out with my friends, I showed no interest in men at all.

Suzy at S.R.S was a true party girl. She went out every Friday, Saturday, Sunday and even sometimes during the week. She and some other girls had begged me to go out one night in July to the place where Suzy had met Bill. I didn't say anything, but I knew Bill was the man God had for me. Suzy introduced us. I danced with Bill only a few times since he was with Suzy.

I saw Bill again the next month in August of 1982. Suzy thought I was nuts when I asked her if she was done seeing Bill. She insisted that he was stupid and not good for marriage. I knew that Bill was a lot smarter than anyone gave him credit for. It was clear that Suzy was done with Bill. It took forever for Bill to ask for my phone number. I found out later that he had just kept forgetting to ask for my number, and I was not just going to offer it to him!

Bill was not allowed to come to my house for a long time. I would never tell him where I lived. We would meet at a friend's house or somewhere in town. I wanted my friend, Russ, to check Bill out to see if he was any good. I made up my mind that if Russ did not approve of Bill, than I would break the relationship off. Russ told me many times that he knew the guys I dated were trash. But Russ approved of Bill. Way down deep, I didn't want Russ to approve of any man. I was scared. So when Bill and I met at Russ and his wife Terri's house for an evening of visiting and playing a few board games, we made a date to go to Bozeman, Montana (about 100 miles away) for a western concert. I think it was Willie Nelson, but I'm not really sure. We all had a good time. It was late when we returned home, so Bill followed me back to my house. We dated for the next two years.

-Chapter Two-

The Marriage

Bill and I saw each other just about every weekend and sometimes during the week, either at his apartment or at my house. Bill was finally offered a teaching job in Ashland, Montana. He broke the news to me one night at my house. I asked him, "What happens now?" At the same time, I was really happy for him because I knew his heart desired to teach children. I told him that I was not going to spend time driving back and forth from Ashland to Clancy, which was about 500 miles one way. I knew how I felt, but I did not know how Bill felt. He hides his feelings quite well. When I was in his arms, Bill asked me, "Well, do you want to get married then?" And I said, "YES!"

Now, understand that Bill and I both had lived alone for about thirteen years. Bill had an apartment full of furniture as well as a car and a small truck. I had the addition, the trailer house, a car, a pickup truck, and a cabin in St. Regis, Montana, where I previously decided that I wanted to live if I remained single.

Bill and I spent the next month not only planning a wedding, but also putting together two households to move 500 miles to Ashland where Bill would be teaching in St. Luke School for the Native Americans. I now see that God's hand was in it all the way. Our possessions sold fast, a lot faster than normal. When it came time for me to sell the trailer and addition, I did not even advertise it. My neighbor across the way called me and asked how much I wanted for it. The next day they bought not only the trailer, but the addition, the metal shed, and any interior that I did not want. My employer even gave me time to move, finish my job, and get married. It was awesome. God even takes care of us when we are living in the world and not even remotely serving Him.

Bill knew that I had a hard time on August 10th because it was my mother's birthday, so he suggested that we get married on that day to create a good memory. (My parents had been killed in a head-on collision years earlier.)

Bill and I married on August 10, 1984 in the yard by the cabin in St. Regis. There were only a few relatives that attended. We had dinner for the crowd at Quincy's Hot Springs Resort. I guess there were about ten or fifteen guests for dinner. Bill did not want to invite his parents, so the guests consisted of my maid of honor, Bill's best man, and a few of my relatives. Quincy's Resort had hot tubs and motel rooms, so we planned to be there for a couple of nights; however, we made it look like we went back to the cabin so that no one would bother us. After we stayed a night or two at Quincy's, we met my Uncle Charles and his wife, Tommie, who helped us move our things in a horse trailer to Ashland, Montana.

- Chapter Three-
The First Teaching Position

Bill drove to Ashland and followed Uncle Charles and Tommie's vehicle while I stayed behind to finish my job four to five hundred miles away from Asland in Helena. I went to Ashland about four or five days later. I don't really think we were in Ashland for the job. Bill and I were hurt emotionally, and both of us were a spiritual mess. We knew that we needed God.

Ashland was a remote town in Montana, so I learned to travel on the gravel back roads to Colstrip to get the incidentals, groceries, medical supplies, and sewing things. On Saturdays, Bill and I traveled one hundred miles to Billings for home improvement supplies and groceries. We were trying to get set up at home and in the area. We really wanted to get established in a church, so we visited a church in Ashland, but it was deader than dead. We went there, and listened to the message. As we walked out of that church, Bill and I looked at each other, and I asked, "Did you get anything out of that?" He answered, "No, I don't even know what the female minister was talking about." I felt the same way. I now know that God was leading us out of religion and wanting us to have a personal relationship with Him.

We never went back to that church. We were still seeking God, but we didn't go anywhere to church. There was a lady at the Native American School who was a Catholic nun, and we talked to her a lot. Sister Joy encouraged us. I didn't know this then, but I'm sure now that she was praying for us.

Since Bill worked at the Native American School, he asked me if we could go to a pow wow. We ended up going to a Native American pow wow a couple times. We even went to an Native American wedding there. It was the most beautiful thing I had ever seen in my entire life. The wedding dress was something else. It was covered with solid beading in blues, reds, and whites. The beads were hand sewn on a white buckskin, which was frayed at the bottom. The headdress was banded with solid beads and matched the moccasins that were beaded as well. It must have taken hours to make by hand. It was truly beautiful. Although we were allowed to watch the wedding, we had to sit on the outside edge facing sideways and were not able to participate at all. However, Bill and I both enjoyed it. It was awesome. To me, it felt like a spiritual experience, but at the same time, I know that there are some things that the Native Americans practice that are incorrect according to God's Word.

Later on the Crow Reservation, we went to another pow wow. It was part of their tradition. We were not able to participate in this one either, but Bill did ask the High Tribal Council if he was allowed to take pictures. He was told that there were only certain pictures that he could take. It was all really interesting because we didn't know why we could take some pictures but not others. We just knew that we had better follow their directions. That's exactly what Bill did, and he took some beautiful pictures. The Native Americans seem to know more about weddings than we do because they handle and respect the wedding ceremony as a sacred event.

Bill's experience teaching at a Native American school was very different because the students didn't want to study or do any school work. For example, the Chief's daughter just went to school and did whatever she wanted to do. She knew she didn't have to study, but that the school had to pass her in her classes. Bill refused to follow this pattern and did not change his values when it came to this girl. But as far as the Native Americans were concerned, they expected him to do that.

There were a lot of changes to the school that year. The school had been established as a Catholic School, then became an Native American School, but was planning to become a Catholic School again. During all these changes they had to dismiss half the teachers, and Bill was not invited back.

While we were living there, we did make friends with some of the teachers. We had a kind of glorified Bible study with them. I mean, none of us knew anything about the Word, and I can only think of one person who was "born again." We were just trying to do the Bible study and had all kinds of questions. We threw questions around back and forth, but eventually stopped the study because it just turned into a time of frustration. We didn't feel like we were getting any answers. I'm pretty sure our friends were aching for God as well. Then when Bill's job ended, we had to hunt for another place to live because we could no longer live in the housing that the teaching position provided.

We packed up all our belongings at the end of the school year. We went on a vacation to California and Oregon to visit my aunt for about a month as Bill sent in applications to different places. We used St. Regis, Montana as our home base. Sometime that month, Bill got a teaching contract in Winnett, Montana.

Looking back on it all, I see that God was always with us and on our side, even when we bought our new car in Ashland. That was a really interesting venture because I had called up the dealership that I had been doing business with prior to getting married. God was all over this, but I didn't know it at the time because we were such a spiritual mess. I made a deal over the phone, then discussed it with Bill, and he said, "Yeah! Go for it!" As I was wheeling and dealing on the telephone, they said that they would deliver the car from Helena to Ashland and pick up the older car. I did all of this from home! It was amazing! I don't know of a dealership anywhere that does that kind of thing without signing papers. We did sign a few papers at the house and then traveled to Colstrip to get all the tags.

-Chapter Four-

Our First Deliverances

On the way to Winnett, Bill and I went to St. Regis and bought a trailer house, which was about eight feet by forty-five feet in dimension. We bought a truck at the same time from my step-uncle. This truck was like a green monster. It had some dents in it, and the trailer, oh goodness! We called this trailer "Monstrosity." It was faded red, had turned pink in some places, and had different tones of silver. It was so ugly that I wrote our name on the front of the trailer with silver roofing paint. Bill just laughed!

We trucked into town on the main street of Winnett in full view of the people who we were trying to impress. Since Bill was the new science teacher for the high school, we were required to have some prestige. The truck looked as if it should be in the car roller derby or something of that sort. But it was quite the truck, and it ran well. We did have a positive appearance with the new car, which looked much better.

We continued to make our presence known by asking where we could park our trailer, and we were told that it should go next door to Mrs. Sulfa's house. Bill and I asked, "Great, but who is Mrs. Sulfa, and where does she live?" Of course, we were new to the town and had no idea where anything was located. After driving around for about an hour, we finally got an idea where Mrs. Sulfa lived and where we belonged. So we parked the trailer house on the lot, which had our back end facing the school.

In the winter, it got really cold in Eastern Montana. It was anywhere between thirty to fifty degrees below zero, and when the snow flew, there was a lot of snow! We set up the trailer house without spending much money, but we knew that we had to insulate the trailer. So we put electrical tape on the water and sewage pipes, wrapped them in insulation, and then wrapped plastic around them. We were able to buy enough baled straw to put a protective insulation all around the trailer's edge. Then we used carpet that we found or that someone had given us, and nailed it around the house. It was avocado green carpet with yellow stains.

To Hippies, Bikers, and Punks With Love

The colors of our new structure clashed greatly. Anyway, our living quarters weren't very pretty that year, but we were blessed.

God blessed us with food for the winter, and He gave Bill a wonderful experience, too. Bill had never been hunting or fishing because his Dad had never taught him. So it was quite an experience for Bill to go hunting with a gentleman named Buster. Buster loved helping people and was ecstatic to teach Bill how to hunt. Buster was Bill's size, but he was rough-looking and an experienced hunter and trapper. Bill shot his first deer with Buster. We bought a small freezer to put in our small trailer. We even made sausage and jerky with the two deer that they shot that year and feasted nicely all winter long. It was so awesome that God fed us, and oh, how I do love venison. In Montana, people aren't paid well for teaching school, even if much is expected of you. Bill was teaching seventh through twelfth grade science and was expected to attend all the athletic games. No one had told us to go to the games; it was just expected. But we didn't know, so we didn't attend all of them. We were not like any of the others in town who were very big on the school sports.

I finally found a job working at a place called a lure house. (I will explain what this is later). I had to wear really old clothes while working there, but I left them at the lure house when I got off work because the stench was so bad! This gentleman and his wife had a business in their house and a building off to the side. If the wind blew just right, it would stink up the whole town! This was not good for our first impressions on the community. I found out later that every person in town wanted this lure house to be gone from their town because of the stench.

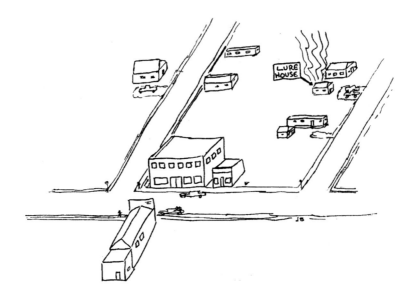

Because this town was small, gossip ran profusely, much like the stench. I can only imagine what they must have said about our trailer house, my husband, myself, or about our lack of participation in the athletic games. I can only imagine! This was a farming and ranching community, and they expected everyone to work as a team. We weren't very good team players because we just didn't know what was expected of us.

Anyway, I cleaned and worked in the lure house and the couple's home. It didn't take me very long to clean because the woman's house wasn't very big. There were just two small bathrooms on the same level. This woman loved to talk a lot, and she asked me all sorts of questions. Well, being the person that I was then, I would just tell her. I was real open and told her a lot of personal information that I should have never said anything about. I'm sure that information traveled all over town because this woman was "gossip central."

As I mentioned earlier, I worked at the lure house, and the couple was right when they told me about my old clothes stinking. When someone is finished working in this lure house, they have to throw those old clothes out because the stench never goes away. Thank God that I didn't have a sense of smell at the time! In a small town like this, it was difficult to find a job, so

I was grateful for the work. My job was to take the old rats and other dead animals that had been laying around for a while, mix them with skunk odor, and grind them up. Hunters would use the different blends as bait to lure an animal like a leopard, a mountain lion, or mink. Then the hunter trapped the animal for its skin. One could earn a lot of money for the skins of these animals. What I did was grind up all of this stuff and use a funnel to push it into different size bottles, then label the bottles. I would clean up the bottles and fill the orders that came in each day. The woman of the house took orders by phone, and then she would give them to me to fill. I learned which lure went for each different animal, the various sizes, packaging, and all about the samples. It was a nasty job, but I got to work by myself. I liked working by myself because I didn't have to be responsible for anybody and didn't want to be around anybody. Frankly, I couldn't stand myself, so how could I stand anyone else? I worked at the lure house when I was needed or when they had orders. It was a part-time job, so I was called in when I was needed and got paid by the hour. I averaged about three to four hours a day, so I wasn't making much money. I changed clothes and showered thoroughly before I left her house each day.

I spent the rest of my time trying to help Bill type papers for school. Bill's job kept him very busy, and much was required from all of the teachers. Bill was teaching six different science subjects at a time, and he was having a hard time keeping up. Bill seemed to fit in pretty well at the school, but I don't believe he was there for the job. I didn't believe it when we were there, and I don't believe it now. I made friends with the superintendent's wife right away. I really enjoyed both her and her husband. I still keep in touch with them to this day. She was interested in sewing, and we got along really well.

On the other hand, there was a Methodist church in town. My goodness, how can I explain it? The church was filled with women that were in strife with one another. The men would also fight with the ladies. They came into church fighting with one another over nothing. We started going there just because it was a Methodist church, and that is what Bill had come out of, so he wanted to go there. Bill didn't drink alcohol, so I decided that I wouldn't either. I thought, "If my husband is not going to drink, then I needed to just go ahead and quit drinking." It didn't make any difference to me if he wanted to go to this Methodist church because it was within walking distance.

The pastor at this church was new, and he was eager to serve God. He had a real heart for God, and his wife was an awesome lady. They had a sweet family with two little girls. There were about one hundred people in the congregation. A fellowship hall was connected to the church, but nothing had been done to it. The insulation wasn't even put in, and no one was using it. They were just too busy fighting. The pastor made a point of visiting everybody at their homes, and he came to visit me. During the visit, we talked about the fellowship hall, and I said to him, "Well, just rise up and do it." He replied, "Well, could you help us if we did?" I answered, "Certainly." I talked to Bill, and he was in agreement with that. So the two "little Bulldozers" rose up and just decided that we were going to do something. So we held a meeting and said, "Look, you need to fix the windows by putting insulation in them, and you need to put some plastic on them." They all argued about it and decided that it would cost too much money. We said, "You can do it with little or no money all." Bill and I figured it out that it would cost about one hundred fifty dollars to fix up the whole fellowship hall in order to use it. We gave at least seventy-five dollars toward the improvements because we felt that it was important.

We finally fixed up the fellowship hall, cleaned up the chapel, and completed the repairs in one weekend. As we started, the others joined us! Bill and I suggested things to do, and the people began to listen and actually do them. For instance, the ladies had a meeting to plan a Thanksgiving social for the Winnett community. I am a "doer," so I have a hard time listening to people deliberating for a long time and trying to make a decision about nothing. I just dive in and do it because that was the way I was trained. But I realize now that I should not expect others to be like me. I've learned that a person needs to focus on being themselves and on God and His way.

Anyway, we sat in this meeting for a couple of hours, and all they did was argue back and forth about gravy! The debate was whether to have the gravy on the potatoes or not. They clucked like chickens in a hen house. That went on for a good forty-five minutes, but it seemed like an eternity to me. Finally I stood up and said, "Ladies, look, why don't you make both gravies, put them on the table, and if someone wants either gravy, they can have the gravy of their choice!" I wasn't very nice. You have to understand that I was born again, but I was still learning. I wasn't seeking God or doing things His way. I didn't know the Word, so I didn't know any better. I continued by saying, "You've argued for an hour and a half and have gotten nowhere! Just do it and be done with it!" There was one lady in particular that turned to me and said, "Dellana, we have been fussing all these years. I want to thank God for you because someone needs to tell us to stop fussing with each other and get with the program." This was a big thing for her to say because she was right in the middle of all that nonsense.

We had the Thanksgiving Social, and it went very well. They used the gravy and my suggestion. I couldn't believe that they did what I told them to do. I mean, there I was, rejected and self-conscious. I didn't even like myself, and there Bill and I were rearranging this whole church and getting these people to operate together as a team. It was amazing because after fixing up the church and having the Thanksgiving Social, these people began to operate in unity. They were happier with one another; that was evident. I was completely amazed at what was taking place. I look back on it now and see that God was using us. I believe with my whole heart that God used Bill and me to help take care of the mess in this church. It was obvious that the church would have died had someone not stepped in and done something. All they were doing was bickering and fighting. Strife destroys. Strife never builds up. Strife never helps anything. It will destroy ministry and unity. There is no sense in it, and it is certainly not God's best.

Anyway, the church started having social events. The pastor invited us to his house for a barbecue, and we started having activities in the fellowship hall. At this Methodist church, we actually had more fellowship than we've ever had at a born again, Spirit-filled, on-fire church. Now I think there is something wrong with that. I believe we need to pray, read the Word, and fellowship with believers. That seems to be God's first priority, so it should be ours as well. The church did turn around, and there were just a couple of people that left. We made curtains, cleaned the church, and kept it clean. We also appointed different people to clean it. It was really good, and I could see God all over it.

During this time, we went to Billings on a Friday night and Saturday for a seminar. A Catholic priest preached and spoke about deliverance. He talked about how God could set you free, and he talked about how God loves you and cares about you. I hadn't heard about this God before. I thought God was like a baseball bat God, that He would whip up on me with a bat if I made a mistake. I mean, I was just "on fire" about what I was learning. Bill was catching it too. We had warmed up the seats of the pew, but we knew there was more to God than what we were getting. Bill had come out of a religious family, and he believed that the devil wasn't real and that Jesus was just plastic. I suggested buying some preaching tapes, so we bought all we could afford at the time. The tapes were on deliverance by Chuck Pearson. We listened to the tapes at least fifty times if we listened to them once. I listened to them to the point where I could preach them by memory.

We were so excited! We didn't know what God was doing, but we didn't care. We just liked those tapes. They were made by a Catholic priest, who I know must have been filled with the Holy Spirit. We recorded the tapes and sent them to Bill's parents so that they could listen to the messages. You know, they were NOT nearly as excited about them as we were. I don't even know if they listened to them, but I'll tell you what, we planted a seed anyway. And we talked about the delivering power of God with them. They just became mad when we talked about it, so we eventually stopped discussing the topic with them.

After listening to the tapes several times, I do remember that I had this vision for Bill. I saw Bill as a four or five year old boy, full of fear in the bedroom closet and trying to hide from his mother, who was trying to get him to wear a "cute" devil costume for Halloween. I told Bill that I didn't think it was right for his mom to force him to wear it, and I understood why he was scared because at four years old, you think differently. Bill thought at that age that his mom was trying to make him be the devil and he didn't want to do that. This had given him a lot of fear at a very young age. We lay on the bed and just prayed in English because at the time we didn't know about praying in tongues. I just held Bill in my arms and prayed with him. He extended forgiveness to his mom, and he was delivered. Praise God that we listened to those tapes and did as we were taught. I mean, God will meet you where you are. I thought it was so awesome because we knew that Bill was delivered from part of his bad experience in childhood.

God is so awesome and does meet you where you are. If you want to be set free from something, God is waiting for you because He loves you and gave

His Son for you. The blood of Jesus washed away a multitude of sins. Just be blessed by God and receive that from Him. This was the beginning of a lot of deliverances in our lives. Shortly after we had listened to those tapes by this priest, the pastor of the Methodist church came to the house. I was so nervous when I invited him in. It was as if I knew God was going to do something in me. The pastor began to ask me questions about my parents' accident and their deaths. I was so torn up emotionally. I just cried and cried as the pastor spoke to me. I kept running back and forth to the tissue box. I thought that this pastor would leave if I did this. Finally, we ended with prayer, and I know there was a deliverance in me that day because I felt relief for the first time with my parents' death. I had godly peace.

The year continued, and Bill worked hard at the school at least fourteen to sixteen hours a day. We stayed very involved with the church. Unfortunately, we found out years later that the pastor and his wife split up. We felt really sad when we heard about it because we knew it was the enemy. But that church, as far as I know, is still thriving and doing well today.

About two months before school was out, the administration notified Bill that they were not going to renew his contract. No one said that Bill was a bad teacher, but it was implied. He really felt like a failure. That feeling didn't really come from the school, but from his past because that was the way he had been treated growing up.

We cleaned up our mess around the trailer house, raked the straw, threw the carpet away, and then took the car and truck. We took off for two weeks to go camping, then went back to St. Regis and worked on the St. Regis home with the money that we had.

Bill drove the truck slowly out of Winnett with Monstrosity trailing in a zigzag pattern behind him. I drove the car. I passed him and drove onto St. Regis. Bill was tired of pulling this heavy trailer down the road. Then he saw Joe's Trailer Sales and pulled in to look at a travel trailer that was eight feet by forty-two feet. God had gone before us, and Joe was actually interested in buying Monstrosity. There was a man in the mountains that Joe had met who was looking for a trailer just like ours. Bill made a deal with Joe for a trade-in for the newer, smaller trailer. So Bill left Monstrosity there and came to St. Regis to get me. We borrowed money from Bill's aunts and returned to Joe's Trailer Sales to purchase the new trailer. We spent our last night in Monstrosity on the trailer lot until it opened in the morning. The next morning, they woke us up, we made the deal and signed the papers. Then we moved some furniture out of Monstrosity and into our new trailer, and set off for St. Regis. It was all God's way and all God's timing.

-Chapter Five-

St. Regis

In St. Regis, Montana, I owned a cabin that I built before Bill and I were married. At an earlier time, my dad placed the thirty-two foot footings for the foundation of their house on this land. My uncles and I moved an addition off of a trailer onto the footing to make a cabin on this property. This was all done after I had lost my parents. Bill and I moved into the cabin and settled there. Bill was struggling to find a job in the small town of around two hundred plus people. I was struggling to find work also. The only good thing about St. Regis was that we didn't have to pay for anything except electricity and gas for the car. We were living off of Bill's last paycheck, so it was tough financially. Bill was on unemployment for a while, and we took on odd jobs. We finally got a seasonal job. We traveled forty miles one way to work at a plant nursery on the swing shift. It was tough for me to work there, but Bill liked the work. The job not only paid for a washer and dryer, but it allowed us to minister and mentor five to ten people. We talked about God with them and were able to take them to a Christian comedian show and a musical event. As a result, a few of them got saved! That long drive to work even allowed us to pray for a car accident victim that was near death. We prayed over her, anointed her with oil, and found out later that she was healed. We put a lot of miles on the car. Bill then went to work for a logger. We eventually met some Spirit-filled Christians in town and met at their motel business for a prayer meeting. One of the ladies there ran the motel and gave me a job cleaning rooms for $1.50 per room.

One night we attended a Bible Study group with these Christians where they asked us if we wanted to be Spirit-filled. That question made me mad because I had been taught as a teenager in a Baptist church that tongues were of the devil. I had heard about the Holy Spirit for the last two years, but was not sure about this praying in tongues business. I challenged these people to prove that praying in tongues was not of the devil by showing where it said so in the Word of God. They showed me verses in the Bible like Acts chapter two, where God had given us the gift of praying in tongues. So we received the Holy Spirit that evening and spoke in tongues. I flat needed it for the deliverances that were about to take place in my life. We attended their group, but the group was not always correct with the Word of God. We didn't know any better. We were just seeking God.

If you wish to receive the Holy Spirit, start reading Act 2:1-4. Actually, the whole chapter of Acts 2 is very good and Mark 1:8. To receive the Holy Spirit, pray this believing by faith that you receive praying in tongues: "Gracious Holy Spirit, Guide, Friend, and Comforter, I ask you in all sincerity of my heart that you baptize me with the Holy Spirit with evidence of speaking in tongues and with the fire, which is the living water of God. Thank you, Holy Spirit. Amen." (Begin to speak out the words or partial words you are getting. The Holy Spirit gives the words and you do the speaking.) This is the fire of the power of God. Praying in tongues is nothing to be afraid of because it is in the Word of God, and it is simply God's prefect prayer through you to God and back again. It is the way the Lord chose to do this.

This Christian group invited an evangelist to town. We went to Plains, Montana to hear him speak, and we also traveled to some other towns for his other speaking engagements. He was a really good speaker. He spoke to us, and he advised us to get out of the group in St. Regis. He came to the house and recommended that we go to Corky Hurst's church in Missoula. So we drove eighty miles one way to church. We disconnected with the group in St. Regis. There was a lot of spiritual paraphernalia that did not line up with the Word of God. However, God was gracious again. Before we officially left the group, they laid hands on me the second time we were there, and they dumped a whole bottle of oil on my nose. I regained the sense of smell that I never had. You see, when my mom was pregnant with me, my dad had a dream three nights in a row that a snake was on his chest and staring at his face, threatening to strike. My dad believed it was the devil wanting to put a mark on me. The snake kept telling my dad that he was going to bite him on the end of his nose. On the third night, Dad said to the snake, "Go ahead, you can't hurt me." The snake bit him and his nose was actually sore for three days. My dad told me that story all the time and said that was why I was born without a sense of smell.

I quit the job at the motel because the salary was so poor. The lady who had hired me had moved to Dillon with her husband to run another motel. I found a job at a truck stop, and the lady I worked for was born-again and Spirit-filled, but she was ROUGH to work for. She was a backslidden Christian. I mean, she would lie to you and tell stories about you. She had me scrub the painted cement floors on my hands and knees and then she told everyone that someone else had scrubbed the floors on their hands and knees. I also cleaned the laundry room and the four showers. My schedule was never the same. Sometimes I worked in the morning, sometimes the afternoon, and even in the evening shift. Sometimes when I did the jobs required, someone else got the credit for it. This lady was just nasty to work for. But at that time, I just grinned and bore it because there was no other place to work. And boy, did the boss lady know this. I worked several jobs at one time, like pumping gas, diesel, propane, selling snacks and drinks, doing the paper work from the mechanic shop and garage, doing the laundry and taking care of the showers. It was a lot of hard work. Sometimes the garage had to take care of wrecks on the local highway pass. It was interesting because sometimes the store would obtain items from these semi-trucks' breakdowns and wrecks. Once we had a truckload of stuffed teddy bears. We began selling those too after I had washed and dried them all. Anyway, that was how the place was run. It really wasn't run with honesty, and that worked against me. The boss lady lied, and that wasn't easy. Once she found out that I was Spirit-filled, things became even harder. Once she accused me of taking forty dollars. Instead of arguing, I just told her that I would pay it and be done with it because I felt that was what I needed to do. I didn't stay there long after that.

After Bill and I left the small group in St. Regis, we started traveling back and forth to Missoula to attend Pastor Corky's church. Pastor Corky changed his name later to Pastor C.A. so that he wouldn't sound like a little kid with big ears. On Sunday mornings, Pastor C. A. preached the Word and talked about the Greek and Hebrew words, how you could get set free, and how much God loved and cared about you. He told us that once you became born-again, you could be used by God. In fact, the very day that you are born-again, you can be used of God. The church in Missoula was an eighty mile drive one way, so Bill and I planned our shopping right around that time. Of course, it was cold enough during the winter that it was no problem. During the summer months, we brought our cooler with us. On Sundays in Missoula, we tried to entertain ourselves without spending money in between the morning and evening church services. If it was cold, then we sat in the mall. When the weather was decent or even below zero, we would have a picnic lunch in the park. There were about two hundred people at the church, and we were rarely invited to spend time with anyone. It kind of surprised me. Pastor Corky and Vikki loved on us a lot. They did invite us to dinner every once in a while. Sometimes we could return the favor and took them to lunch after church. They discipled us and cared for us. Pastor Corky's main message was "Pray, read the Word, and fellowship with believers." I don't know how many times I'd ask a question and the answer would be "Pray, read the word, and fellowship with believers." I kept thinking, "What does that have to do with the price of tea in China?" I understand it now, but I didn't then.

The church was like a warehouse with cement floor and metal chairs. We finally did obtained a piece of rug to put up front where Pastor was preaching, but for a long time, when you were out under the power of God, you were on a cold cement floor. Most of us were so desperate for the Word that we sat in our cold metal chairs with our coats on. I did get some material on sale and made about fifty pillows for those hard metal chairs, which everyone enjoyed.

At this time, Bill and I were between jobs. I was sewing my own clothes, and Bill was making leather goods as a hobby. I don't know what we would have done if we had to pay rent. We both got up early in the mornings. I would take my Bible and go pray in the Spirit and read the Word at the same time. I was told later that you couldn't do that, although I was doing it the whole time.

For the first six years at Sonlife Church in Missoula, I was just a mess. I mean, I was so angry, so mean, and so ornery. I'll just never forget it. I just read the Word all the time, I would pray, and then I'd dump out my emotions on other people. Yet Bill and I both saturated ourselves in the Word of God by reading and listening to teaching tapes. We just did it all the time.

I'll never forget the second time that we went to cake and ice-cream night, which was what Pastor Corky called the Sunday night services at Sonlife Church. This was like dessert from the Lord where people could receive freedom, forgiveness, and emotional healing. I noticed this lady that was across the building. I had been praying for a friend and a sister in Christ to come into my life. I remember Pastor Corky saying to me after that night, "Dellana, if anybody would have stopped you, you would have killed them on your way over to Judy." I knew that this was the sister I had been praying for. Judy and I spent a lot of time together. She was about two years older in the Lord than I was. We spent a lot of time praying together. Eventually this church went down to about twenty believers for some reason or another. I have no idea why because I was so protected from that and was not a part of any mess in the church. I found out later that Judy had been praying that the church situation would not affect us. We were totally sheltered. When the church went down to twenty people, I really felt bad for the pastor and Vikki. But, I tell you what, this man really preached the Word and God's love and deliverance. He was very much an encourager. He was a wonderful pastor for Bill and me.

I had never seen anyone fall out in the Spirit before, and I didn't know what it was. One Sunday night, Judy fell down on the floor, and I asked her what had happened. She told me, after giggling at me, that it was a time of deliverance in God. I told her that if it was God, then I wanted that experience too. She was so easy to talk to, and we got along great. This woman Judy was a character. I mean, she'd wear one red sock and one green sock, and a green skirt with a yellow blouse, and all the colors clashed. She wasn't very pretty, but I tell you what, this woman was beautiful to me on the inside. If anyone said anything against Judy in front of me, I was in their face telling them to leave her alone or deal with me. I was really protective of Judy, and she was protective of me. It was a God-ordained relationship. There was such a unity between us. We would pray for someone or something, and it would happen immediately! It was very cool and very God.

Bill and I were little bull dozers again and went into Judy's trailer house to help her clean it up and get everything working. I don't know how we did it, but we gathered enough money for a new hot water tank, heating tape, insulation, and we got her heat back on. Unfortunately, her hot water heater burned out again because she didn't call us until two years later to check the heat tape and replace it as we had told her. I wanted to give again and help out, but God would not let us. God said that we had a good giving nature, but He wouldn't let us do anything more for Judy. It absolutely broke my heart, but it was good for both of us because it taught me to be obedient to what God wants. It taught Judy to obey what she was told and to use wisdom in dealing with her house. From that day forward, my husband Bill, thank Jesus for him, said, "If God says to give it, do it, but make sure it is God." So Bill keeps me in check to this day. Praise God! I love to give!

Anyway, after Judy went out in the Spirit that one Sunday night, I went home and prayed. At that time, I was so hungry for God that I spent one to five hours a day every day drenching myself in the Word. I was thirty six years old and a mess. I told God, "If you don't fix me, I'm going to die!" That week, I continued being saturated in the Word and building up my faith, so I believed that I could be slain in the Spirit myself the next Sunday.

That Sunday, I was so fidgety and couldn't sit still because I knew that God was going to answer this prayer. Pastor Corky looked at me toward the end of the morning service, just before dismissing the people and said, "Dellana, God has something special for you tonight." I thought, "I want it now! Right this second!" He made me wait until Sunday night. And I had to listen to the teaching all the way through that Sunday night. I was already out of my seat and up in front when Pastor Corky gave the altar call. I operated with so much impatience! How childlike I was and still am! I fell out in the Spirit that night. The first thing God showed me was Lady and Sheba, my pets that I owned that had died years before. I was playing in an open field of flowers in God's throne room with my dogs. When I got up off the cold cement floor, I felt such a peace instead of the grief I had felt before over the loss of my pets. I asked God how I was different. I could see the difference in myself during the week at home.

The second time that I fell out in the Spirit, I saw Jesus along with the six guys who had violated my body when I was eight years old. I saw the six guys standing in front of Jesus, and I saw Jesus. I was eight years old again, standing behind Jesus, and peeking out from behind His robe. Jesus said, "I need you to forgive these boys." I said, "All right, as long as You're here, I'll forgive them." I was out a long time on the floor, and I was doing a lot of crying. In fact, I was on the floor several times in those six years just crying. Almost all I did was cry during those six years, but it was a good six years. I really was delivered in a lot of areas. When I got off the floor that second time, I knew that I knew that I knew that I was different. And I thought, "God, You've got to show me how I'm different." I pressed myself into God so much that I did not care what way He set me free. I just wanted FREEDOM!

I know it doesn't happen like that for everybody, but I pray that everyone will press into God and know that He loves them and will meet them where they are. God has a tremendous loving hand to deliver. He cares more than any mind can grasp. Sometimes it is being put out under the power of God, sometimes it is repenting over some things, sometimes it is believing the Word that had been revealed to you, sometimes forgiving others, but it is all deliverance and well worth whatever you have to do. We need to have our mind renewed to the truth of the Word. You have to have your heart open if you want deliverance.

When I was eight years old, my parents and I lived on a farm. Mom and Dad used to go to card parties with the other local farmers. When the parents got together, the kids would go along to the events also. Some children would go to sleep or play hide-and-go-seek outside if it was fairly nice, and some played games in the house. I know the children were not allowed to bother the adults, when all of us were at the card parties.

Anyway, we were playing hide-and-go-seek outside. Everybody had gone home except for these six guys and me. The guys were fifteen, sixteen, and seventeen years old. I remember the two older ones, but I don't remember the rest. They were curious about sex and how it worked and all that kind of stuff. I was the only girl left, so while we were playing, the guys grabbed me and ripped my clothes and my pants partly off and laid me down on the frozen, snow-covered ground, and one guy got on top of me. There was one guy holding my arms and the others were holding my legs apart. Another guy was trying to rape me while another had his hand over my mouth. It took all six to hold me down because I was fighting that hard. The one guy that was going to get on top of me had an erection, and it had started to touch my genitals. All of a sudden, my dad and mom were leaving, and my dad whistled. I got up and put on what was left of my clothes. The boys scattered. How I ever hid that, I don't know. But I got in the car that night, and I was too scared to tell my parents. I mean, I was eight years old; I didn't have anything be attracted to. I was plump, and my breasts hadn't even begun to develop. I hardly knew what sex was and had no idea what had just happened, but it really frightened me. I just felt dirty, ashamed, guilty, and put down after that. I guess I covered everything up with my coat when I got in the car. The boys hadn't ripped my pants, but they ripped my blouse. I don't know how I got rid of those clothes. Mom never noticed that my clothes were torn. I guess I just threw them away so she wouldn't notice. I never told my dad or mom until after my first husband had died. From eight years old until I was eighteen and was about to be married to my first husband, the incident never came up. I kept it all to myself.

After that traumatic event, I remember that I would wear clothes that covered me completely and blame myself for what had happened as if I had encouraged it in some way. I would not look at anyone to say "hi." I would not go to dances or parties. I would not stay after school. I hated walking home alone even in the daylight. It was an awful, tormenting thing, and it was my fault or so I thought. I would not make friends. I still struggle in the social realm a little, but God has helped me a lot.

I was so angry. From that day forward, when I went to school, I didn't have anything to do with anybody. I acted in anger and that kept everybody away from me. I was terribly frightened. Thank God I did not have to continue to go to school with those boys. Later on, God told me that it was a direct attack from the enemy to steal the anointing that God had for me to walk in.

As we were going to Pastor Corky's church, Sonlife, God repeatedly slain me in the Spirit, and I wanted God to move as fast as He could. I asked Him to, and He honored that request. I finally asked God to slow down a little, and He honored that request as well. I thought, "Who is this God that talks to me and answers me?"

The third time I was put out on the floor, Jesus was there, and I was again eight years old hiding behind Jesus. Jesus had me come in front of Him. There were several different times that He walked me through the violation of my body. I remember that no one actually penetrated me, but it was a fearful enough experience to be quite traumatic for an eight year old. The Lord took me in stages each time I was out in the spirit. Finally, Jesus had me stand in front of Him and forgive the guys. Several times out in the Spirit, I went to each guy to forgive them and gave them a hug. I did all that and every time I got off the floor, I would ask God, "How am I different?" I noticed that I had less and less anger each time. And after the whole thing was over, a lot of rejection had left. Guilt, shame, rejection, and anger. Anger is just an outside emotion for an inside hurt. Those emotions of fear that caused anger were stuffed inside me, and God brought them out into the open. Then forgiveness came.

To prove that God's forgiveness is the greatest forgiveness you could possibly ever do, God had me intercede in prayer for the main guy that had tried to rape me. I prayed for him, and God gave me compassion for him and one of the older guys. I mean, I had such compassion for the older one. God showed me that he was married and had two little girls that he was molesting. I prayed that the girls would get out of that house and be protected, that the lie would be exposed so he could get help because he needed Jesus. I had such a compassion for them. That is the forgiveness of God, for there is no one that could do that on their own.

In my previously angry state, I had been terrible to my husband as well. I mean, I would scream and holler and throw spoons in the house. I even threw cups on the floor and broke them, only to have to clean them up later. I remember after one of the fights that Bill and I had, I went out on the porch. It was springtime, and there was a flock of butterflies. Bill had gone to the lake to get away from me, and I sat there just crying my eyes out and asking myself why I ever got married. All of the sudden, the Holy Spirit said to me, "Look over to the left." There was a whole mess of butterflies flying around, and as their wings opened and closed they were saying, "I love you, I love you, I love you." It was all together like great music coming from those butterflies, and I knew it was God saying that He loved me. That just made me cry harder. Bill finally came back, and we went off to do something together. Bill was different that day too and had changed for the better.

We didn't have a lot of money, and that didn't help the marriage situation either. We were adamant about going to church on Sunday. I mean, we'd go without food if that is what it took. No one ever knew we were in this financial state. We didn't tell them. We'd pray sometimes for people to invite us to lunch so we could eat because sometimes there was not always food in our house. I remember one time Bill said that we couldn't go to church because we had no gas money. I was terribly upset, and I just fell apart. I don't know why I had to squall and bawl to God to get what I wanted, but that was what I was doing. I prayed and cried out for a way that we could go. The next door neighbor, Bonnie, came down and said, "God just told me that I needed to bring you twenty dollars and some food." She brought in about four sacks of groceries. We took the twenty dollars that Saturday afternoon and went to church on Sunday. We went into church Sunday, never said a word to anybody, and just praised and thanked God that it all took place and that we got to go to church.

-Chapter Six-

Deliverance

Before I ever met Bill, there were three years straight when people who were close to me died. I was twenty four years old when this three year period started. It was about every three months that I found myself in a funeral home. There was no time to grieve one death before there was another one. My dogs even died during this time period. At this time in my life, I was loaded with loneliness, rejection, sorrow, and grief. I was totally run by my emotions, not by the Spirit of God. Lady, the dog who was sixteen years old; Sheba, who had been my dog; and my grandma, my mother's mother, all died in Nebraska about the same time. What hurt so badly was that I was never able to say good-bye to them.

Grandma had taught me to crochet. She was funny, and I enjoyed her to the max. She had leukemia. My dog Lady had gone up on a hill behind the house to lay down and die. I don't know how Mom noticed Lady with all that was going on with her mother, but she did. Mom took Lady and Sheba to the vet and had them put to sleep. Mom was by herself, and I wish I could have been there for her. It wasn't very long after that that Grandma died. I was relieved that she didn't have to suffer any more. I didn't want the animals to suffer either. But I never had a chance to grieve.

My first husband was the killed in a drowning accident. It took fourteen days to find his body. There was a discussion about fake funerals and other ridiculous things, so there were a lot of past things I still had to deal with emotionally. I now know how that spirit of rejection operates. I believed many lies from the enemy that were rooted in rejection! What started as a mole hill as a child had increased and become full blown mountains as I grew older. During this time of losing loved ones, I was so distraught that I wanted to kill myself. The only thing that stopped me was the thought that if I killed myself, I'd go to hell, and I didn't want to go there. Is that not God?

There were about twenty six deaths during that three year period. I lost my animals, my grandmother, my first husband, my grandfather-in-law, my father-in-law, my mother-in-law, and all of my first husband's family during this time. It added sorrow and grief upon grief. I was living in Salem, Oregon during these three years in the 1970's. When the gas wars were going on, I decided to move back in with my parents. Gas was hard to get then in the city, and we had to wait in long lines to get a limited amount. It was not the same if you lived off the beaten path. I was working in data entry in Portland, Oregon, which was forty miles one way from where I lived. After the two other key punch operators quit, I had to take over their work. Since I was doing the work of three people, I asked my supervisor for a raise. I gave my two week notice when they told me that there would be no raises at this time.

I called my dad in Helena, Montana. My parents and I had a special relationship. My mother was not just my mother, but my best friend as well. She corrected me, she loved me, and she cared about me. She not only spoke those words to me, but she acted like she loved me. Now, she taught me a lot of old wives tales as well that are totally incorrect with the Word of God. God showed me that later in my life, and I repented of them and let them go. It doesn't matter where incorrect words or thoughts come from. If they are not in agreement with the Word of God, which is the truth, then we must get rid of those thoughts.

My dad was a harsh disciplinarian and very strict. When he told you to do something, you better be doing it. He didn't believe in telling anybody anything more than once. He was terribly impatient, full of anger, full of resentment, and looking back, he probably needed to issue a lot of forgiveness. He believed if you wanted anything done right, then you should do it yourself. At the same time, my dad had a real giving heart. Mom and Dad were constantly doing things for other people. We often had misfits on our doorstep. You name it, and we would help out people and counsel them. I can't tell you how many marriages Dad probably saved and the many people he helped to turn around. I remember my dad reading the Word of God out loud to me when I was four years old as I went to sleep in his arms. I don't know why I didn't interpret that as love from him. Maybe all his screaming and hollering and carrying on at me blocked me from knowing that he did love me. I didn't know my dad loved me until I was eighteen years old. All those harsh words canceled everything positive out. At the same time, I really didn't feel I had anybody but my mother and dad.

We lived on a farm in Dore, North Dakota near Fairview, Montana, and everybody worked hard on that farm. We worked from daylight to dark most of the time and in all kinds of weather. In Eastern Montana, it can get cold, and it snows a lot at times. I remember several different times that it was three or four days in a row, fifty degrees below zero, and it had already snowed six to eight feet a few days in a row. I was walking across the fence post and just having a great time trying not to fall into the snow. You couldn't stay out long in that kind of weather without proper clothing. We had a whole week of snow like that one time. Usually it was thirty degrees below and we still had to go to school, but you would dress appropriately for that. I could tell you story after story.

We ended up delivering lambs in March, practically the coldest month of the year, and I can remember having lambs all over the kitchen. One time Dad was sick with the flu, so Mom and I had to lamb the ewes. Mom and I brought this little lamb into the kitchen, and Mom remembered Dad giving lambs whiskey to warm them up, so she gave the lamb a full shot of whiskey all at once. The lamb gasped, went stiff, and died. We laughed about that, and my dad came tearing out of the bedroom madder than a hornet. Mom and I just laughed at him. But he was mad understandably because each lamb was worth anywhere from twenty to fifty dollars at the time. He corrected us saying, "Yeah, a couple of drop of whiskey, but not a whole jigger!" That was pretty funny, and there were a lot of times like that with Mom and Dad. Like I said, Mom was like my best friend, and I had a lot of respect for my Mom and Dad. We were in unity with one another. But Dad would make fun of someone's actions to correct them. All it made me feel was inadequate. God had to heal the bruise that it left in my heart, and I had to forgive Dad.

Eventually, the farm had several crops go bad because of weather, and we lost everything. We finally had an auction and sold everything off. We were in debt when we left the farm. I had traded two lambs that I had raised to get a bicycle. I offered to help my parents by sell-ing my bicycle at the auction of the farm. So they sold that, too.

As we left the farm in debt, my dad was very downtrodden. I was in the second part of my seventh grade year, and I had done well in the first part of the year. Before that, grade school was terrible for me. From that time on, I went to seventeen different schools. To this day, I don't know how I made it through high school. I had stopped being around anyone. I didn't want to have anything to do with anybody. I rejected them before they could reject me. I was operating in anger, rejection, and unforgiveness mainly be-cause of the attempted rape in my childhood. A few years passed, and Mom and Dad ended up living in St. Regis, Montana. Dad tried working in the construction business for a number of years. He had been on unemployment and started doing odd jobs around St. Regis. Mom cleaned houses for people and also began doing odd jobs. One day when I was thirty years old, they drove thirteen miles away to Superior, Montana for an ice cream cone. On the way back, a girl passed in a no passing zone and hit them head on.

Before the wreck, Dad, Mom, and I had been having dreams about a car. I had been having a dream about a car wreck on and off for about five years. I would dream about a car wreck that occurred from a car passing another delivery truck in a no passing zone. There was a large delivery truck that no one could see around or see over. Someone would pass this truck, and I would wake up crying because it seemed as if the car that had been hit was carrying people that were close to me.

My dad acted differently for a year before the wreck happened. One day, my mom said that we needed to go to Missoula, about eighty miles from St. Regis, to add my name to the checking and savings accounts. So I took off of work that Friday in May and went to Missoula. Mom and I spent the whole day together, and we laughed, shopped, and had lunch; we just had a wonderful and glorious time. We did everything we had done in our lifetime in one day. Mom let me know that there was five hundred dollars in cash in a file box in the trailer house. When we went back to the restaurant to pick up my car and say good-bye, I went back and hugged my Mom two or three times. She said, "Dellana, what is the matter with you?" I just started crying and said that I didn't know, that I just felt like I wasn't going to see her again. She said, "Oh, don't be silly." I cried part of the way home to Helena as well.

I had worked as a key punch operator for the highway department for almost seven years, and the girls from the office and I went out for drinks that Sunday night. I came to work with a hangover on May 9, 1977. At 2:50 in the afternoon, I was key punching and a picture of the car wreck dream flashed in my mind. I started to cry a little because I had the car wreck dream flash in my mind, and at 3:10 in the afternoon the phone rang, and it was the police. They told me to go down to the police station. I asked, "What for?" I thought that I might have done something wrong. I was told that my parents had been in a car accident. I asked if they were all right. He did not answer me. I asked him again, "Are my parents all right?" He finally said, "No, they are not all right." I almost fell to the floor. I said, "Both of them?" He said, "Yeah, both of them." I got off the phone and fell apart telling my supervisor that my mom and dad had been in a car wreck, and I had to go to the police station. Thank God she was smart enough not to let me drive. My roommate who worked at the highway department drove me to the police station.

I walked through a corral fenced area and then through glass doors into a room that was enclosed with glass where everyone could see me. I sat on a hard wooden chair next to the girl who brought me. She had no idea what to do with me because I was such a mess and just sobbed. The policeman came in and told me Mom and Dad were hit in a head-on collision. Mom was pinned under the steering wheel and was killed instantly. They took Dad to the hospital in Superior and twenty minutes later, he died. I was really upset that Dad died in the hospital because he hated doctors. He wouldn't even go to doctors.

The car had been driven way off the road and looked like an accordion. The fishing gear, vacuum cleaner, shampooer, and all that stuff had been shoved forward. Mom always carried at least one hundred fifty dollars in her purse; that was gone. There were a lot of things from her purse that seemed to be gone. I never got any of the cleaning supplies back either. I always wondered what happen to them. So here I was, an only child who lost both of my parents in a car wreck. Now I felt more alone, more rejected, more devastated, and I didn't care whether I lived or died. It was like my insides were turned completely outward. How hard that was to bear. But somehow I went on.

The woman I was with drove me back to the trailer house where we were staying in Clancy, about 25 miles from Helena, and I started calling people. I called Charles, the youngest of Dad's brothers. He was silent on the other end. It took Charles quite awhile to answer me. I am sure it was a shock to him, too. I called Bob and Fran, who were my friends who lived in Boulder about 15 miles or so away. When Bob came to me in person, he had me drink a straight shot of whiskey; it didn't even phase me. I didn't even taste it, and I hate whiskey.

Bob and Fran drove me to St. Regis. I left the car, and I cannot tell you how I got my car to Clancy. I had called a whole bunch of relatives and had asked Charles to pass the information on because I didn't have Mom's address book until I arrived in St. Regis. Fran and I couldn't quit crying. Bob asked, "Girls, are you ever going to stop crying?" I said, "I don't know."

Previously, Bob and Fran had stayed with Mom and Dad for a good six months in St. Regis. My parents were good to Bob and Fran, who were some of the misfits on their doorstep. My parents were like parents to Bob and Fran as well. As they took me to St. Regis, Fran asked if I had called any of my mother's relatives. I hadn't. I'm glad Fran told me to take my address book with me before we left town. We stopped late in the afternoon. Bob made me eat a cup of soup. I would have rather thrown up. Then I called some of Mom's relatives.

Bob and Fran stayed a couple of nights, and then they had to go back to work. When I called Bob to tell him what had happened to my parents, he was tearing out the door to see me and forgot to bring Fran. He drove about seven miles before he remembered Fran and had to go back to get her from work. That helped as some light humor on the way to St. Regis. I don't know how you can laugh and cry at the same time, but Fran and I seemed to be able to do this together.

Anyway, we got to St. Regis and, of course, the relatives started pouring in. On the way, we had stopped by to see an old boyfriend of mine that I had previously broken up with. I knew I really shouldn't have done that because he wasn't any good for me, but I just needed someone. He came to St. Regis and took one of Mom and Dad's cats. When we arrived at St. Regis, one of the two cats was hiding in the bedroom while the other was looking out the kitchen trailer window just screaming. She seemed to be looking for my parents. My old boyfriend took that beautiful Siamese cat. He stayed for a week or so. The relatives came in, and Fran and Bob came back and forth to check on me. It was a mess, and it felt like a zoo with all those relatives. The trailer house was eight feet by forty-five feet; the addition was ten feet by twenty-six feet. There was a big freezer in the addition to the left of the door as you entered the room, a cast iron wood burning stove, and no room for any more people.

Fran came to me and said, "Dellana, they are taking things out of the trailer house without consulting you." So I thanked her for telling me, and I went in and sat on top of the freezer and told my uncle Charles that he knew that he had been appointed to help me with this. He acknowledged that he knew about the agreement with my Dad and Mom. I asked him to gather up all the relatives and bring them in the addition. I had already gone through some of Mom and Dad's things. The five hundred dollars that Mom told me was in the file cabinet was gone. The hundred pounds of flour, sugar, and various other things that my parents had stocked up on were gone.

I waited until everyone sat down and said, "Look, I am my father's daughter. Your fault, my fault, nobody's fault, these things that you have been stealing, you're going to bring them back into the house right now. You haven't asked for them. You are stealing them. My dad told me that you'd act like this, and I just couldn't believe it! It makes me want to vomit. So you go right now and get all the stuff."

I waited a few minutes while the different ones retrieved things from their cars. I continued, "From this day forward, if you want something from here, ask me. If you don't have the decency to ask me and you must steal it, then get out of here, now! Do you understand me?"

Everybody's eyes got big as I screamed all of this. I said, "I want to let you know too that there is five hundred dollars missing out of a file box that my mother told me about. I think I know which one of you took it , and you just keep that." I said, "I hope it reminds you everyday that you're a thief. If you think you need that money worse than I do, you just keep it. There are a lot of expenses in burying one person, not to mention two at once!"

I never got the five hundred dollars back, and I am certainly not sure how people can live with themselves having this kind of behavior. I just dealt with the thievery. Right away, Aunt Mary piped up and said, "I want this lamp." Aunt Clem joined in and said, "I want this." Aunt Mary piped up again and on and on it went...

The whole thing makes no difference now. I forgave them a long time ago for that nonsense. I still don't understand how people can be so incredibly callous and cruel. I have found this to be so in every situation dealing with death.

My uncle Charles and I went to Missoula several times to make all of the arrangements. I went to the funeral home first. I had already made up my mind that since the law hadn't changed for burying people on one's own property, I was going to bury Mom and Dad myself. I made arrangements in Superior, listed the homestead as a grave site, and planned to follow the necessary guidelines. Harold, who my dad had helped to build an A-frame, lived just up the hill from their place and had a back hoe. Harold back hoed the graves, and Dad's brothers built the corral fence around the grave site. There is a permanent grave site in St. Regis where I have a grave plot and room for other family members, plus Harold and other family if they wish.

Anyway, when I arrived at the funeral home in Missoula, the people were trying to sell me two eight hundred dollar caskets, which supposedly were the cheapest ones. I already knew that I needed to ask for welfare caskets.

They have welfare caskets that the state issues, which were about two hundred dollars a piece. And that was what Mom, Dad, and I had decided on prior to the accident. When I asked for welfare caskets, the funeral home director freaked out and so did Charles. I was moving on and running stuff, so they either had to listen to what I said or I was going to go to another funeral home. You have to understand that I was mean, nasty, and upset, so I was quite the boss. I told the funeral director how to shift money from Social Security and the Veterans Administration so that I could pay the difference. In fact, between both Mom and Dad, Social Security, and the Veterans Administration, the funds were more than the funeral bill. The funeral director just freaked out and said that I just couldn't do this. I said, "Yes, I can do this, and this is how you're going to do it!" The funeral director eventually followed my instructions.

We waited for forty-eight hours, and I took full charge knowing all the rules of burial. We went back from there to distribute possessions, combat thievery issues, and work through arguments between brothers over a gun. I had to deal with many emotions and other people's childish behavior at the same time.

It took six to eight weeks to separate the trailer house from the addition. We moved the addition over to the footings area and built another ten feet by twenty-six feet structure to make a cabin in St. Regis. We hauled the trailer four hundred miles or so out to Clancy, Montana where I sat it up with an addition of ten feet by twenty-six feet , which Charles, Albert, other relatives, and my boyfriend had built for me. Thank God that Mom and Dad had some money in their checking and savings, and that my name was on it so I could have a place to stay. It was about eight to twelve weeks until I finally went back to work, and it was awful. I could hardly stand to be at work. Of course, I had a lot of issues with the girls there. Most of the issues were in my own mind. I imagined them talking behind my back all the time. I was just a spiritual mess.

I am so grateful to God for the deliverances that started six years later during what Corky called "cake and ice-cream" time from the Holy Spirit on Sunday nights at Sonlife Church. God started taking me to the throne room one Sunday at a time for one deliverance at a time. This was when I was reading and studying the Word over long periods of time. God put me in the throne room with my mother and dad. At first, I didn't know which one to go to and which one to grieve over the most. So, finally God separated them and took me into the Throne Room with my dad, and we dealt with that first.

When I came up off of the floor, I wasn't as angry, and I didn't have nearly as much rage. It was as if I had just grieved over my dad's death, and I had peace. I thought, "God that's really awesome. How did You do that?" He said, "Just by showing you that they are all right." I don't know to this day if they were born again or not, but I have peace with my dad's death. I got that peace by allowing God to rearrange my thinking through the Word. The Word of God says to set your mind and keep it set on things that are above, not on the things that are on the earth. I decided to do that. I decided to cast down vain imaginations and think on those things that are good and lovely. God had a hope and plan for me. So, while I was devastated and wanting to kill myself, I let the Word of God change my thinking, and I confessed the Word of God several times a day until my mind was thinking things that were good and lovely instead of stinky!

I made up my mind to memorize Scripture, and it was hard because I had a hard time remembering my own name. I laid down all that guilt and rejection, one thing at a time, then I went into the throne room of God where He put me out on the floor. The next few times that God put me out on the floor, I had heard the preaching and teaching of the Word of God, and then He showed me my mother. That was really a hard one. Man, it was hard to turn the pain loose. But, it was almost like Jesus took my hand and said, "She is all right." I walked down a path and visited with her and loved on her and cared about her. This was an example of what God can do if you will let Him. Do I still think of my parents? Yes, but it is with peace. I still miss them on occasion as well. God chose to put me out on the floor several times for several reasons to fix my inner being.

One time I was out on the floor and was with Mom and Dad together. Each time I would get up, God supernaturally gave me peace in my heart. Somewhere along the line, the hurt for those twenty six people disappeared as well. Did the deaths happen? Yeah, but I don't have any grief. The rejection is gone, and so is the sorrow. God used Mom and Dad's death to set me free from sorrow, grief, and particularly rejection. Each time I got off of the cold cement floor, I asked God to show me how I was different. I saw that the anger was gone. I quit throwing spoons around and stopped breaking cups. I quit being so angry and mean to my husband. I began to believe that I could trust God.

> "Lean on, trust and be confident in the Lord with all your
>
> heart and mind, and do not rely on your own insight or
>
> understanding" (Proverbs 3:5).

I believed, finally, that God loved me. Was that a hard time that I had gone through? Yes, it was very hard because I felt so alone and empty. But after being with the Lord, I knew that the blood of Jesus had set me free. And now I just want that same freedom for others. So I pray with all my heart that this story is touching your inner heart.

I know that anyone can be set free and made new on the inside if they decide with all finality that the Word of God is alive, true for them personally, and is willing to get into the Word and be filled with the Holy Spirit. For when Jesus died on the cross, a little over two thousand years ago, He took every sin, and wiped it away. The Word is true.

> "But seek (aim at and strive after) first of all His kingdom,
>
> and His righteousness [His way of doing and being right], and
>
> then all these things taken together will be given you besides"
>
> (Matthew 6:33, Amplified).

-Chapter Seven-

Lolo

After St. Regis, we went to Lolo, Montana. We found a trailer lot in Lolo where we lived for three years. It was good living in Lolo because it was about fifteen to twenty miles out of Missoula, so we could do more things. I also met up with Debbie, my old friend from the motel in St. Regis. She was working at a convenience store. I started working for Debbie, and I worked my way up to assistant manager for a year and then manager for another year when Debbie moved up to another position in Utah. There were three different stores that we spent time praying for. One was in Lolo, one in Missoula, and the other was in East Missoula. Each one of the stores had satanic garbage around them that needed to be run off. God used Debbie and me to pray that stuff out of there. Debbie and I met on a weekly basis to pray for all the needs of the store.

I worked in the store at Lolo usually from 11:00 PM to 7:00 AM. Most of the time, I either cleaned or waited on people. At those hours, we'd get a lot of strange people coming into the store. One night I remember a guy coming in, and he was just really weird. I started praying in tongues out loud, and he started talking about some really weird stuff. I thought he was going to come behind the counter. I took authority over the devil and told him out loud to shut up and get out of my store. I kept telling him to get out, and he finally did. I wasn't thinking about the risks and went out after him. He went around the edge of the building and disappeared, and I never saw him again. I later shared this experience with Debbie, and she confirmed it. To this day I do not believe it was an individual. I believe it was a demonic presence. It took me quite a while to get over that incident. It did seem like the store had more peace after that happened.

It wasn't very long after we left that convenient store and went to Missoula. Our prayers were answered. Debbie had a really good team that she brought from Lolo to this store on Russell Street. They were hard workers who showed up on time. There was a satanic priest living a block and a half from the store. Right across the street, there was a place where satanic worship was taking place. Thank God the store closed at midnight, but you could hear their worship from the store. Down the street, across from the priest's house were more grounds where they had satanic rituals. There were a lot of children that were missing in that area. I know from what God told me that there were human sacrifices with human blood drinking. At that same time, we were praying things out of Missoula. Bill and I were still attending Sonlife Church and were getting stronger in the Lord. We were going through more deliverances and changes. Bill started substituting everywhere around the Missoula area and worked at a grocery store at night. They put him as the head of cleaning the meat department, and he had to hose down and clean up while being in charge of four or five younger employees. Bill didn't like it much, but it was a job. Bill was working night shift and working during the day. Sometimes he went two or three days before he could get some sleep.

I was working swing shifts and night shifts several times when people didn't show up for work. In addition to that, I worked morning shifts for Debbie two days a week. We were still going to church on Sundays. Oddly enough, we both were off on Sundays most of the time. We would work at night and sleep in the day, and I cannot tell you how many times people called us and woke us up. They'd wake us up at 8:30 AM and wonder why we were not up yet. We could never get it across to others that people who work at night need to sleep during the day.

A lot of times, Bill and I would wave to one another going to and from work. It seemed like that happened a lot, and it went on for a long time. It was frustrating, but Bill and I were still consistent with being in the Word and going to church. I was also around Debbie, who was Spirit-filled. Because of all the satanic practices around it, the convenient store on Russell Street had manifestations of the evil one on the outside of the building. There were some kind of worm-like creatures crawling up the building, and when Judy (my friend from Sonlife), Debbie, and I prayed over that store inside and out, those worms died and fell off instantly. There was a tremendous amount of thievery in that store before we moved in and prayed. The church and Judy stood in agreement with Debbie and me and prayed with power in unity.

Sonlife church went down to twenty believers, but we operated in unity, in godly unity. We accepted everyone just like we were. We were all a bunch of outcasts that had come into the Kingdom of God and were desperate for God and for His healing power.

I guess Michael was one of the people who were most precious to us because he had cerebral palsy. Apparently when he first came to Sonlife, before Bill and I met him, he was so small that he could lie down on a portion of the love seat, and someone could sit at his feet comfortably. He grew to at least six feet, two inches and could sit up on his own in a wheel chair. God had been healing him. You could tell. We'd get him out of that wheel chair and walk him around believing for his healing. We'd see the manifestation of God, and we would set him back in the chair, and his speech began to improve. As people screamed at him, Michael would say that it wasn't his ears that needed healing, but his body. God really moved on Michael's behalf in the realm of physical healing. Michael was about 24 years old and very smart. Michael is still in the wheelchair and lives in Missoula to this day.

Anyway, the church stood in agreement with us for the store and for all the satanic paraphernalia to be cast out. We found out later that two and possibly three different areas in Missoula were targeted by satanic worshipers as three of the places of their pentagon. Judy and I spent hours and hours praying over this neighborhood and praying against the satanic priest. If he wasn't going to get born again, he needed to get out of town. There was Christian comedian at that time, Mike Warnke, who came in to do several concerts. The convenient store told us that we were not to put up any posters. Debbie and I prayed that the management wouldn't see it and that whoever needed to go to these concerts would see the poster and no one else. We placed the large poster low in the window, behind the magazine rack along side the front door.

The satanic priest frequented our store. He was about seven feet tall, and he bent over to see the poster. He looked like a long-legged giraffe with his butt up in the air and put his nose right up against the window to see what this poster was about. It was hilarious. Debbie and I just roared with laughter. He came into the store and we had to watch him because he would try to steal stuff, and we had to take authority over it. He never could steal anything. Debbie and I were usually there together when he came in. Well, the poster stayed up and the management never noticed it, and not even the district manager who came to inspect our store noticed the poster.

There was one time that God instructed Judy and me to drive around the whole block seven times and claim it for the Kingdom of God. Then we were to shout the praises of God. Two days after that, the satanic priest moved, and there was no more satanic worship there again. We have no idea where he went. We do know that he went to Mike Warnke because Mike talked about the satanic priest being there and pointed him out. Mike did preach the gospel to everyone at these concerts. He was awesome; we really enjoyed it. We had his tapes, too.

When we moved from that store, we moved to another area where there were not only more satanic practices, but hard core bikers and homeless people. It was as if God moved us deeper into enemy territory. I could feel it. I mean, I would go to work happy and get there and feel nasty. There were a lot of bugs and worms on the side of that building that left when we prayed and anointed it. It was very dirty on the inside and outside. When we were cleaning out that store and moving in, there was a great big bookshelf that was three feet taller than me. Debbie moved it out so that we could rearrange the store. That bookshelf almost fell on me for no apparent reason. We took authority over that. We started pleading the blood of Jesus and taking authority, although we really didn't know to plead the blood of Jesus at that time. God still protected us and ran that evil stuff off, too.

I worked as a manager for a year at that convenience store in East Missoula. It was really hard for me to be a manager without the aid of an assistant manager. I didn't enjoy it or like it, but it was a really good training ground for me. Bill continued to work at least two jobs. We finally did manage to pay off a truck and the car and get a second car for Bill to save on gas.

We had the trailer house, the addition, and a metal shed with a picket fence. We were working hard for the money. I would get up at 2:00-2:30 AM in the morning and be at work by 3:30-4:00 AM to run the store, and I'd be there until 7:00 or 9:00 PM. I would only write down part of my hours because if I wrote all of them down, they would probably have fired me. I was on a salary, and any time that I worked over fifty hours would be extra money. I was working about seventy hours a week, and when I'd finally get a day off, Bill would take me to St. Regis and I'd sleep the whole time. I mean, we hardly saw each other. I was doing a good job, but it was really tough and demanded long hours.

I really struggled when Debbie moved to Denver. I was happy for her because it was an increase in pay. But I told her, "I'm happy for you to have a job in Denver, but I just don't feel like you are going to stay in church." She was supposed to go to Denver, but it changed to Salt Lake, Utah. She had just gotten back in church again, and she and her husband had split up. I told her that I had traveled all over the country and found her and would keep her as a friend. I intended to stay in contact with her, but I said that I would write her one time and that she needed to respond to me. I just prayed that she would get into a church. I remember going to work one day and just bawled my eyes out. God said, "Release her; let her go." So I did. I don't know where Debbie is now. I pray that she is in God's hands.

One time in prayer, God spoke to me about getting rid of Mom and Dad's oak table and chairs. I didn't want to because I really wanted them. The Lord started showing me that they weren't my table and chairs, but Mom and Dad's. As a result, my keeping the table and chairs had kept the grief alive. The Lord was really sweet with me. He guided me to a second hand dealer in Lolo to leave the table and chairs there. The man at the antique shop acted like they were just perfect, and they weren't. He bought them from me and set them in front of the antique shop. Just a few days later, God told me to drive by the antique shop. I saw the lady buying the table and chairs as the Lord reassured me that they were in good hands. For several months, while I was in prayer, God dealt with spirits of grief and set me free. The Lord showed me that keeping things from the past as memories can sometimes cause spirits of grief to linger if we relate the object to the loss of a person that was dear to us.

Bill and I were working hard but still not making much money. We were getting a firm foundation by being in the Word, getting deliverance, and being at Pastor C.A.'s church. One morning as I prayed on the way to work, I told God that I didn't get enough time with my husband. I can look at it now and see that it was God because I was a mess, and Bill was a mess and we needed to be apart. But I was frustrated and wondered if this was all there was to life. I asked God, "Isn't there somewhere else we could go or something else we could do to make more money?" Montana is a beautiful place, but the minimum wage is so low. The church was not moving either. We were asking people to come, but they were not coming. It just seemed like everything was at a standstill, like a rodent spinning on a wheel wanting to get off.

I felt in my spirit that God wanted us to sell everything and move back east. I asked God to give me three confirmations. I didn't even say anything to Bill. When I arrived at work at 3:30 AM, the night person said to me that I didn't seem too happy as a manager. Then he asked, "Where are Bill's parents? Are they back east somewhere?" I said, "Yes they are." He said, "Why don't you just sell everything and move back east?" I thought, "Well, that is confirmation number one." My second shift girl came in, and I was upset over something. I don't remember what it was but she said, "Dellana, aren't Bill's parents back east?" I said, "Yeah." She said, "Why don't you just sell everything and move back there? You don't have to put yourself through this torture." I thought, "All right, that is confirmation number two." A girl came in for the 5:00 to 9:00 PM shift, and while I was visiting with her for a little bit, she said, "Have you ever thought about moving back east and just getting rid of the store?" That was confirmation number three.

When I went home that day, Bill was laying in bed awake. I was glad to see him. I asked if he had to work that night. Bill said, "Yes, and I was thinking we're working too many hours." He asked if I would be willing to sell everything and move back east. I laughed and told Bill that I had just been in prayer and tears asking God if He couldn't change our situation. I told Bill about the three confirmations. So we agreed to give our notices at work on July 4th. We knew it was God.

Lolo

I gave my two weeks notice as a manager, my last day being July 4th. I was given a party with balloons and flowers. It was nice and unexpected. We did sell everything we owned. It was the end of July when we moved. We divided the stuff up at the trailer house and what we didn't want to take with us, we took to St. Regis and left it in the cabin. I knew this was all God because we put the trailer house up for sale, the addition, and the metal shed. There were a lot of tools, all our furniture, and a lawn mower that barely ran.

God had told me to call Bob and Fran to see if they wanted the truck and car, and they bought the Truck and the old Subaru. A lady metal artist came and bought the trailer, the freezer with the addition, and the metal shed for a fair price. We shipped clothes and sewing materials ahead to Bill's parents; left the large tools in St. Regis; had some timber cut on the St. Regis property; and sold the lawn mower for twenty dollars after a multitude of questions, all within twenty to twenty five days.

We headed off to Maryland to start a new life with the Subaru packed with personal items and camping gear. Everything was paid off with the exception of the private bills we owed Bill's parents and aunts. We had about five to six thousand dollars from all the sales. We took our time traveling the fifteen hundred miles to Maryland. On the way to Bill's parents, we had a small vacation and visited some relatives of mine.

-Chapter Eight-

Moving Back East

On the way to Maryland in the summer of 1991, it was obvious that even though Bill and I had good Bible teaching, had gone through deliverances and was being used by God, we still had far to go. God is indeed faithful to complete what He began. Spiritually speaking, Bill and I were a mess and were in need of more healing.

Bill was raised in a fear-filled home. He came into our marriage with a fear of failure. That meant that everything I said or did, he interpreted it as rejection and a fear of failure. It was hard for him to get or keep a teaching job because of his fear. He worked as a substitute most of the time, and his emotions were really messed up. God has set Bill free from a lot of different things and is still working on him.

Bill had emotional baggage, and I sure had a lot of emotional baggage, too. That baggage was really fighting with one another. We were both only children. The enemy lied to him about a lot of different things, and he lied to me about a lot of different things. When we grow up in the world and don't have God, we receive a lot of hurts and thoughts from the enemy that simply are not the truth.

I was rejected to the max. I wouldn't look at people when I walked down the street. I was very uncomfortable if we had any social gatherings. Whether they were Christian or non-Christian, it didn't matter. I really didn't like social gatherings at all. I felt that I was not only rejected by people, but by God himself. I had a lot of self-pity, pride, and unforgiveness. My mind was continually busy worrying about stuff and trying to please people. I had learned a lot about who I was in God over the last six years, but I still had a long way to go.

I was a work in progress. I didn't think that I would ever get along with any female and have a healthy relationship. I knew that I needed to because that was God's plan. We serve a God of relationship. I knew that I was a perfectionist. If I didn't do everything just right in sewing, I'd throw it out and start over. I would then feel like I was a failure and no good. I didn't even feel like I was worthy enough to be married. I was too fat, too ugly, too thin, or too that. I felt like a misfit.

One time, I invited all the people from Sonlife Church to come to my house in St. Regis. We all hung out there. I tried to accommodate everybody and do what I needed to do, but there seemed to be a lot of issues. I thought I was to blame for the issues. I was so concerned about people not liking my house and was concerned about not having a door on the bathroom, just a curtain. I had so many bad feelings about the whole thing and about the people. That was all part of the rejection. When we were in St. Regis and Lolo, God began to show me some Scripture.

> "I have the mind of Christ. I think on those things that are
> good and lovely. I have total recall in the name of Jesus Christ."
> (II Corinthians 10:5)

I began to say those promises two or three times a day. Every time that I noticed that I had a thought of fear, I'd say that Scripture.

> "My speech is filled with grace, seasoned with salt so that I
> know how to answer every man's question." (Colossians 4:6)

I knew I was too blunt, and I was too up front. I claimed this verse and said it often. Now I know that God created me with a gifting of boldness, and I just acted in that. I didn't know that my perfectionism was related to my gifting of diligence. I didn't know that there was honesty and integrity in my actions. But it sure needed to be all refined by God. I wanted God to take the rough edges off of me because I was so blunt, so I claimed His Word to help me and refine me. I needed to learn to keep my mouth shut sometimes and not just speak my mind when I wanted to, which I believe is called "self-control." God has brought me a long way and has refined my bold speech greatly. God now uses me in that area a great deal.

Another Scripture that God took me to is "Greater is He who is in me, than he who is in the world" (I John 4:4). I had a hard time remembering peoples' names; I even forgot their name as soon as I was introduced to them. I could hardly remember my own name, let alone anything that anybody told me. If I sat in a group of people who were talking about current events or history, I wouldn't understand a thing they were talking about. I'd sit there and grin and bear it and be bored. Once in a while, when I opened my mouth and asked about it, I felt lower than a snake's belly. No one would have the kindness or patience to explain it to me. I can understand why now because I was impatient and angry. I would fly off the handle a lot of different times. Bill had to put up with that. He didn't know what to do with me. The sad thing about this was he blamed himself. It wasn't him at all. It was the excess baggage that I came into the marriage with.

I pray that I can now share my story with others so that they can be delivered from their baggage. We hurt everyone else, as well as ourselves, when we don't seek the Lord and ask Him to help us identify and get rid of our wrong emotions. We need to turn away from our sins and ask the Holy Spirit to help us identify why we act the way we do, and then show us hurts in our past that we need to be healed from and forgive those who hurt us. Another Scripture God showed me was James 1:5:

"If any of you lacks wisdom, let him ask of God, who gives to all liberally without reproach, and it will be given to him."

And I needed godly divine wisdom! In order to be healed, I needed to spend time meditating on the Word. I quoted it until I remembered it. I knew I needed the Word of God to survive. I also somehow knew that I needed to pray the Word. Pastor C.A. spoke on praying the Word. It is a requirement of God.

There is a scripture in Proverbs 3:4-6 that I memorized, too. Some of the main verses that helped in my deliverance were Colossians 3:8–9, Matthew 21:21-22, and Mark 11:23-24. When I prayed against these mountains of pride, rejection, or loneliness, I believed in faith that they would be removed. At the same time I was taught to put on the armor that God gave me everyday (Ephesians 6:10-18). I still do that today and everyday. I am not leaving my house spiritually naked!

"But now put away and rid yourselves completely of all these things" (Colossians 3:8). One morning when I was praying and reading the Word, I saw this verse and started crying. I said, "God, I've got everyone of them except for lying. Where do you want to start?" He began to deal with the anger, and He dealt with the rage, and we got some of that taken care of. The bad feelings

I had towards other people, gracious! I would cry at the drop of a hat over nothing. I just couldn't seem to quit crying. Later on, the Holy Spirit said, "You do have a problem with lying." I thought, "Oh great, then I've got all of them!"

God showed me that the slander, foul-mouth abuse, and shameful utterance from my lips had to go. When I was at home, I'd talk about other people in just terrible ways. I was gossiping, and that is slander and foul-mouth abuse. So was swearing and most slang expressions. I shut those things down. We listened to tapes on the Book of James that told us how our words and confessions are important. We need to line up with our confessions. I wasn't doing any of that. I told God that I didn't want Him to take off just the outside layers of my sin. I wanted Him to get to the roots of the problems, where they all started, especially the roots of anger, rage, and bad feelings towards others. I was so touchy, and just the littlest things would set me off. I was no bundle of joy to say the least.

It helped me to know that God said that I am a royal priesthood, part of a holy generation, and that God loves me. Jesus died on the cross a little over 2,000 years ago to set me free. He died on the cross to set me free of anger and bad feelings toward others. Every one of the feelings I had, Jesus had on the cross. There was so MUCH! How He could carry my junk, my husband's junk, and every person's junk from the beginning of time, to now, to the end of time. He took on each and every one of our emotional baggage; each and every one of our sicknesses and diseases. I looked at that truth and realized that I needed to praise God, rejoice, and confess the Word out loud. I needed the Word. I needed to be Spirit-filled, to have the Holy Spirit reveal truths about the Word of God. I needed the power of the Holy Spirit, which includes all that He has for today, for now! I needed the correction.

The Holy Spirit revealed to me that some of these bad feelings I had toward others were not anything I imagined they were. Some of that anger and rage was from the rape. I took on shame and guilt, and it was multiplied to the point that I assumed everything was my fault. If I walked into a room and somebody was talking, I was positive they were talking about me. The Holy Spirit asked me, "What makes you think that they are always talking about you?" I said, "Well they are, aren't they?" He said, "No, they are not, not every time." And He said, "They really want to be friends with you, but you're unreachable." That had impact on me, and I knew it was pride on my part. I realized then that if I wanted to have friends, I needed to make myself friendly. So when the enemy would lie to me and tell me I was rejected and alone, I would tell the enemy, "The Word says you are a liar, so thanks for telling me I'm NOT rejected and alone." You see, I had trained myself to recognize the voice of God and the voice of the enemy, so I learned how to rebuke the lies of the enemy in my mind and receive God's truth.

-Chapter Nine-

The Chocolate Year and a Half

We did get to Maryland after visiting many relatives and friends. When we arrived in New Windsor, Maryland, Dad and Mom greeted us as we came in with our sleeping bags, etc. They parked us in the bedroom, and they invited over a few friends and relatives I had not met.

It was hard having a relationship with Bill's parents. I tried to build a relationship with them, but it was impossible. We did the best we could. There was a lot of fear, rejection, and loneliness there, too. Every time I would work in the kitchen, I could never do anything right. I used the wrong fork, knife or plates. I didn't set the coffee cup in the saucer at the right side of the plate, the glass wasn't where it needed to be set, and I was just trying to please them. When I washed the dishes after the meal, Bill's mom would imply that I didn't wash dishes well enough. I did the best I could. I tried to bless them, and I cleaned the house while Bill and I looked desperately for work.

Dad and Mom would take us out to dinner, as our money supply was not good at the time. Dad would set up arguments about where we would go eat. He'd take hours trying to decide where to eat; by the time we were getting to where we were going, it wasn't worth the effort. One time in particular, I remember he wanted to go to Benihana's. I asked, "What is Benihana's?" He said, "It is a Japanese restaurant where they cook the food in front of you with trained chefs." Everyone was explaining what it was, and I said, "Well that sounds like a great thing to do. Let's go." Then Dad became mad, and I couldn't figure out why. It seemed so stupid to me. Dad said, "We should just go to the pizza place or Burger King instead." We finally settled on some family restaurant, and I had no idea what was going on. Bill was livid, and I didn't understand why he was so mad either. I do remember being disappointed and thinking the whole conversation was pretty silly and unnecessary.

I found out later that we weren't supposed to pick Dad's suggestions if it cost a lot of money, even though Dad offered in the first place. I suppose that we should have guessed that. Bill was upset because his dad tried to embarrass him in front of me. Bill and I went to Benihana's years later. Frankly, it was not that expensive, so I really do not understand what all the fuss was about, but then who needs to understand the enemy and his ways?

We stayed at their house for about three weeks. One morning, Dad and Mom started arguing. I had no idea what they were so upset about. It was so strange to me. Actually, Mom and Dad woke Bill and me up with their loud discussion. I asked Bill what was going on. He said, "Pack your stuff." He was real mean about it and just kept saying, "Pack your stuff, we're going job hunting today." Bill went out of the bedroom, and there was a full blown argument between his parents. I was dressed by this time and trying to do my hair. I had no idea what they were talking about. Bill kept hollering at me, "Pack up the sleeping bags and all that we have, and let's go." So I began packing. Bill came back into the bedroom just fuming and rushing to pack while telling me to pack. We quickly put it all in the car.

Dad yelled at us on the way out with the last load, "Bill, don't leave angry. Come back, and let me buy you a suit." I had no clue what that was all about. I don't recall what Bill said to his dad, but he was pretty nasty. We left and went job hunting. After Bill calmed down, he told me that his parents were mad because we were in the house for three weeks, and they had it in their minds that we were going to stay there the rest of our lives and sponge off of them. That certainly was not our intention. We never said that or thought any such thing. How embarrassed Bill must have been. We had about fifteen hundred dollars left from the Montana sales. Bill was so angry and upset that he started taking it out on me. I fought back rather harshly because of the hurts and anger from my own life. Finally we calmed down.

Bill knew he just had to forgive his parents and let the anger go, but he said that he was too mad to forgive them for anything. He asked, "What was that suit thing about?" I said, "I don't know, that argument was the strangest thing I ever heard in my life." I told Bill what they did was not right and that I was sorry that he had been treated that way. I said, "I am sorry that they made you feel like a failure and no good, but that is not true; that is not what God says about you." He said that we would go back for the rest of our things later, but we were getting out of there now.

We camped somewhere in Pennsylvania and prayed about where we were supposed to go. We felt like we were supposed to be in Hershey, Pennsylvania. We thought that was where God wanted us, but probably most of our decision was made out of the flesh because Bill was determined to get out of his parents' house.

We began apartment hunting, and we found a small apartment up two flights at a nice apartment complex. There was a bedroom, a small kitchen, and an open area that made the nine hundred square foot apartment complete. We didn't have any furniture, so in this case, small was good. We could also have our dog and Samson, our ferret. It took most of the fifteen hundred dollars that we had to rent this place. We put a deposit on the apartment, and since we were out of state and had a Montana driver's license, they requested a reference. So we called Dad Zabel. I really believe God took over in this case. Dad Zabel came up to meet us there so that he could sign the reference papers. They accepted his reference because the manager of this apartment complex's dad was friends with Dad Zabel. This man was a Methodist pastor who Dad knew. I thought, "If that isn't God…" Bill knew it was God, too.

We had very little money left to rent a moving truck and move everything from Dad and Mom's to our new apartment in Hershey, Pennsylvania. Dad tried to help move us up those two flights of steps, but I sat him down when I noticed it was too much for him. Dad and Mom gave us a bed and a dining room table with six chairs. That furniture about filled the apartment with the sewing machine in the living room. There was a neighbor who was a weight lifter that noticed us moving in, and the man helped us. It was certainly another God-send because we did not know how we were going to get some of the heavy stuff up the stairs. Dad was still talking about giving Bill a suit. Bill stood his ground and said he didn't want it.

We still didn't have jobs and had no prospects of any job. We had met a man named Randy back in Montana who asked Bill and me to bead earrings and sell them to the western shops in the east. We had no TV or money for entertainment in the apartment, so we played games, studied the Word, went to the auction house, hunted for a church and jobs, and beaded earrings. We would travel to the western shops and would get accounts from businesses that wanted to sell Randy's earrings since he was in Montana.

It got to the middle of the month, and we had applied everywhere we could. It became apparent that we were the "outsiders." I applied everywhere for a data processing job in which I had experience and training. No one called. Bill and I both redid our resumes and spent the money we earned from the earrings to copy those resumes and letters of reference. I began to apply for anything: cleaning houses, baby sitting, and being a nurse's aide. We did get one job from a bid that I put on cleaning a house. It was a giant house, and it took six or seven hours altogether to clean. That was good because we did it every two weeks. We were fired after a while. I have no idea why. Maybe it was because Bill and I were working together. That hurt.

The bills would come in regularly, and Bill and I had a practice of setting them by the door and praying, "God, You've got a problem. You sent us here, and Your Word says that You'll take care of us." The money would then come in from the earring sales, a part-time job, selling a sewing project, Bill's aunts, Bill's mom and dad, finding money on the ground, gifts, surprises, etc. There were even a few times that an unexpected check could come from an over payment or something we did not know about. That happened every month for close to a year. God is good! I don't know, but this place seemed very highfaluting. I felt as if everybody was looking their noses down at us.

Bill went down the street and got a job working at the grocery store. He walked in and told the manager, "I breathe, hire me!" He was the meanest man Bill ever worked for! Bill couldn't satisfy his boss no matter what he did. He'd work night shift, day shift, mid shift, anything. I finally landed a part-time job at a car dealership doing odd jobs in their service/parts department. The scheduling of times varied, and there were not many hours scheduled during the week.

We lived in Hershey for about one and a half years. Bill only worked at the grocery store for about three months until he got a job at the chocolate factory in the warehouse. Bill tried to get the manager of the grocery store to let him come in one hour later so he could work both jobs, but that manager was not having any part of that. It was difficult to get a job in Hershey unless you knew someone. We knew that we were supposed to work at the Milton Hershey School. I put in applications as a custodial worker, house parent, office worker, etc. Bill put in applications as a teacher and a house parent. We had qualifications for that and references, but they lost our applications every time we submitted them. They lost both of our applications several times, and we finally gave up. We prayed about it, and we knew God wanted us there. But circumstances blocked us. People and circumstances can get in the way of God's perfect plans, so God will adjust the plan to take care of His own (Jeremiah 29:11). We somehow were able to make ends meet financially, but it was difficult. I remember one night it was our wedding anniversary, and Bill and I thought it would be nice to celebrate by having some seafood. A restaurant was out of the question, but Bill thought we could go to the fish market and purchase some fish. I told him we had no money for it, and I took the dog for a walk. When I returned upstairs, Bill felt like he was suppose to take the dog for another walk. He came back upstairs all excited because he had found a twenty dollar bill on the ground at the bottom of the back stairs. We went to the fish market and purchased seafood and had a fine anniversary dinner that God had provided.

Once again, we found ourselves traveling a distance to church. We felt that we should attend Lifeline Church in Lebanon. We felt like we were supposed to be there and many in the congregation wondered, as we did, why we were there. The church was born again, Spirit-filled, but they were subdued about it, and we had to dress a certain way. It was kind of silly, but at the same time, you could see they had hearts for God.

-Chapter Ten-

A Whole Lot of Lebanon Bologna

We went to Lifeline Church and met Abby and Bob. They asked us about where we were living, and we told them that we were hunting for an apartment that was a little cheaper. They offered to rent an apartment to us that was located above their shop. I asked, "What kind of shop do you have?" She said that she sewed and sold second hand clothes on consignment. I said, "Oh, you're somebody that I could learn sewing from." She said, "I don't know if I am a very good teacher, but I'll help you if I can." They said we could rent the apartment for whatever we thought we could afford. I said, "Well, how about we rent it for three hundred dollars a month?" Abby had a funny look on her face, but Bob said, "Yeah, that's great."

So we rented a moving truck and moved from Hershey to Lebanon, Pennsylvania and rented the apartment above the shop. It was a lot bigger than the other one. The bedroom was really big, and the living room was a good size. It wasn't level, and the floor was somewhat like a roller coaster, but there was a good size room off of the living room, which was perfect for our sewing room/office. The kitchen was long but needed some attention. Bill and Bob fixed it up together, and it looked really nice when it was finished.

We were somehow able to get out of the lease in Hershey. I don't recall how, but we did. I do remember cleaning the apartment thoroughly and having them inspect it. We got back our cleaning deposit with the exception of fifty dollars. Apparently they kept that no matter what. Anyway, we got into our new big apartment. The ferret's cage fit in there really well, and Samson, the ferret, had plenty of room to run. The big windows let in plenty of light for my sewing. It was nice.

It was nice having a place to sew because I had to make clothes for my work. I had already left the Ford Dealership to go to a video store in Hershey; then I went to Lancaster, Pennsylvania to work at a trade school. This was a school that offered boys and girls a last chance before they would go to jail. They would stay in dormitories. I was a part-time dorm director, and I moved from dorm to dorm. There were four dorms in all with different rules for each dorm. It was a rough place to work, and there were many challenges for me, from always having to wear make-up, to students lying, to planning activities, to having to find a way to get to and from work through the snow storms. They even wanted me to play Santa Claus. I said, "No."

It was good that we were settled at this apartment, even if I had to drive quite a distance to work. After a couple of months of renting from Bob and Abby, we raised the rent ourselves to three hundred fifty dollars because we wanted to be fair. They did pay for the heat and air which sounds great, but that meant that they controlled the air and heat from the downstairs thermostat. This led to some very cold days and nights in the winter, not to mention very hot summers. We were thankful to have a cheaper place to live.

It was an older apartment with "talking banisters" that made noise when the heat did come on. Bill and Bob worked out a plan for the new kitchen. We found some cupboards and redid them. Someone gave us a counter top that was actually too long. It was perfect because Bill used the extra material to make a table for the microwave alongside of the kitchen stove. Bill did a wonderful job on the kitchen. Everything came together by praying each piece in, and we got it done. We needed some laminate. We were driving by a garage sale that the Holy Spirit sent us back to where we found the perfect piece of laminate in the color we wanted. God is good!

We kept going to Lifeline. We met quite a few interesting people, like Craig who had been in a car wreck and was supposed to have died twice.

Once he did die and came back to life. He was also paralyzed at one time, and when we met him, he was walking. He improved constantly as he kept confessing the Word of God over himself. He had a metal plate in his head and was a real giver who just walked all over town. He walked over eight miles a day. Bill and I really enjoyed making friends with Craig.

I kept inviting Craig over to the house for dinner, and he would never accept. One day I put my foot down and told him that he was going to come to our apartment for dinner on a certain night and what we were going to have, and Bill would go get him. He did finally come over that night for dinner and confessed to me that he was afraid to come. Apparently he thought I could read his mind and knew everything about him, and that scared him. Of course, I couldn't read his mind. Craig finally told me that it was my "anointing" that actually scared him and made him think that about me. Craig later helped me understand that when I thought people didn't like me at the trade school where I worked that it was because of the God on the inside of me. People felt like I could read their whole life because the Holy Spirit would reveal some things to me.

In Lifeline Church, we met many people who were babies in Christ. I just prayed for them, and God showed me they were starving for the Word of God, and they were going to die if somebody didn't do something with them. God showed me in a vision a human skeleton that had mold and cobwebs over it as I prayed for them in intercession. It broke my heart because it broke God's heart. I just felt impressed to start a Bible study teaching the basics of faith from the Word. We met at Chris and Barb's house. Chris was a biker and was sold out to Jesus. Barb was a lover of people with lots of hurts in her life. Their gifting was hospitality, so they loved having it at their house. We would meet either Friday or Saturday depending on the availability of the day. I made the mistake of telling them they could call me anytime, day or night, and they did that. Unfortunately, they usually called while I was trying to study and pray for the weekly lesson. I started teaching them about faith. We had praise and worship and talked on scriptures about faith. Sometimes I'd take an old tape that I had recorded from Pastor C.A.'s church. I also wrote back to Montana and requested copies of all the sermons and said I would buy them.

The study grew. People were getting born again and Spirit-filled. People were getting healed physically and emotionally. They were falling out in the

Spirit. I would pray for people and anoint them at the end of each meeting. Everybody smoked cigarettes. There were more hippies than bikers at the Bible study group. That went on for a really long time.

One guy wore a three piece suit, and everyone in the church graciously welcomed him. The next Sunday he wore a nice shirt and clean jeans, and they wouldn't acknowledge him. This gentleman came to me and asked me, "Why am I good enough in a suit and not in my jeans? I am the same person." My response was that I was sorry that he was treated that way; that it wasn't right but he had to forgive them and go on. I reminded him what the Word said, "Don't judge them," but pray for the leadership. This was done a few times in this little Bible study for babies in Jesus.

The elders, deacons, and pastor at Lifeline heard that I was doing a Bible study. The elder assigned to this problem did not call me. Instead he called Barbara, the host of the Bible study. The elder was assigned to come to the Bible study to make sure I was teaching Biblical principles. But as soon as Barbara got off the phone with the elder, she called me. She said that an elder was going to come to the Bible study Friday night and check me out. I asked, "What do they want to check me out for?" She said, "He wants to see if you're doing what you need to be doing according to the Word of God." I said, "Is that a fact!" She replied, "Yes." I said, "Doesn't make any difference to me, but thank you for calling me and letting me know because now I'm going to pray and see what God wants me to do." I prayed, and God had me change the plan from hearing a tape to teaching a message on the armor of God. I can now see this is the sort of thing that usually takes place when someone is getting results with the Word. I did wonder what impact the armor of God had on this elder that night; only God really knows.

We had praise and worship that Friday night and had fellowship. Then we went into the Word of God. As soon as I was finished, I said, "Okay, Louis, what did I do wrong?" I figured that was what he was there for. He said, "As far as I can see, you spent a little too much time fellowshipping after praise. You should have just gone straight to the Word." I was surprised that was all he said. I replied, 'Thank you, I'll take that into consideration." He was amazed because there were a couple of people I prayed for that night that fell out in the Spirit and that didn't happen too much in Lifeline Church.

Bill was rarely able to come with me to these Bible studies. I wished he could have, but he was working at six or eight little schools around Lebanon as a substitute. He also worked at Sears. Sometimes he couldn't even go to church. We were fortunate in that we could walk to church from the apartment as we only had one car for awhile. We stayed in the apartment for almost two years until we had enough of the air/heat situation. So we started apartment hunting in Lebanon. We found a small apartment building just up the street. It was the same price as Bob and Abby's, and we had more privacy. We moved into the back apartment on the second floor and eventually were able to move to the back apartment on the first floor after we prayed it in. The apartment turned out to be in the perfect area because I started a new job three blocks away, so I could walk to work.

Strangely enough, it was another convenience store. God had told me that wouldn't have to work in another convenience store unless I wanted to. However, my friend Clara seemed like she needed help at the convenience store she worked at. I talked it over with Bill because the Lord had asked me if I would consider working in the convenience store with Clara. I decided to take the job to help her out. So I quit the job at the trade school and mostly worked from 4 PM to 12 midnight for five days a week. Sometimes I'd help out on other shifts, but they were fairly regular hours. It turned out that I eventually made more there than at the trade school because of the cost of travel and time it took to go there.

One night, in early November, a guy came in to buy a Snickers candy bar. I had a really odd feeling on the inside of me. I had a really bad cold, but I also had a funny feeling about this guy. I went in the back and smoked a cigarette, and I kept coming back and forth. I kept rebuking the thoughts of fear that were going on in my mind. I had fears of being robbed, but I kept fighting those fears. I don't know why I didn't pay attention to those feelings, because I never had them before. I went out to wait on the guy with the candy bar. He came to the counter behind me and when my back was turned to ring up the sale, he jumped over the counter, wheeled me around, hit me in the face three times and broke my glasses in pieces. I had already closed the till, and he was ticked off about that. I had my long hair up in braids on the top of my head. That all fell down. He flung me around like a rag doll and was beating me up. He kept punching me in the side. Apparently he was a

Vietnam vet who needed some drug money. He continued hitting me and then jerked me up to the till on my knees. He ordered me to open the till drawer. I couldn't see the keys as he was yelling at me to hurry up. He started hitting me some more. When I did get the drawer open, he took the money out of the register and then took the heavy metal money-order machine, which weighed about fifteen to twenty pounds, and hit me over the head with it. He was trying to kill me at that point.

When all of this was happening I was screaming. It was strange, but on the inside I could hear the Spirit of God saying, "What are you screaming about?" I replied back, "Yeah, why am I screaming?" It was like I was talking to myself, but I couldn't get anything out. I really thought this guy was going to kill me. It was the oddest feeling I ever had. I couldn't think of any scriptures; I couldn't think of anything to say to him. On the inside, all I could think of to say was "God, God, God."

Finally he left the drawer open and made a mess behind the counter. Blood was everywhere. I lay on the floor. I believe he thought I was passed out, and I wanted him to believe that was the case because I didn't want to die. I know that God protected me that night. Finally, I heard the bell on the door ring. I thought that meant that he had left, so I got up and started running to the door. At the same time I was walking to the door, the police pulled up out front. I opened the door with my hair streaming and blood going everywhere. He asked if I was just robbed. I said, "Yes sir, he's going around the edge of the building. Go get him! Go get him!" The policeman didn't go after him, but he came inside with me. I couldn't figure out why he didn't go after him. I kept screaming for the police to go get him and they didn't. I was screaming and praying in tongues at the top of my lungs out loud in front of this policeman. He wasn't trying to ignore me or be kind; he honestly never heard me. It was very strange, but I knew it was the Lord's wrath.

I tried to call my husband. The policeman wouldn't let me call. I kept telling them to call my husband, and they finally called Bill. I told them that I had to call my district manager and my manager. They said that they would take care of all that, so I gave them the phone numbers. They made me sit still, and I put a rag over my nose to try to stop the bleeding. They called an ambulance.

Before this robbery, God had me praying for the police department. He had shown me during prayer that there were quite a few police there who were dishonest. Now, I was still praying in tongues very loudly as I got into the ambulance. It was as if they didn't hear me. They just ignored me. There were no facial expressions that would even hint that they heard me. I mean, I was screaming! We got to the hospital, and they took me to the examining room. I was still screaming in tongues. There were two police officers that were standing at the far door about one hundred feet away. I said, "God, they are dishonest, You told me they were dishonest, and I don't want them in my room." It was as if they couldn't enter that door. They turned around and left. I just laughed and that hurt, and I continued to pray and screamed in tongues again. The doctor came in and asked me some questions. I answered them and continued to pray loudly in tongues in front of the doctor. I mean, I was really upset with the enemy! I did finally settle down. Bill showed up and, of course, I fell apart. He wanted to know if I was all right. Bill was white as a sheet when he realized that this guy wanted to kill me. The very thought that he may of have lost me was all over his face. I will never forget that look.

The recovery was rough. I had to go to the convenient store doctors; I couldn't choose my own. I had to go on this convenient store's workman's compensation. They didn't want anyone off work very long. Strangely enough, I had prayed just before this that I'd have Thanksgiving and Christmas off. I did!

I was sore for a long time. I needed help getting off the toilet, getting in and out of bed, and getting up and down the stairs. The financial situation was such that Bill had to go to work. So Bill put the phone by me in case I had to call him. Bill bought me a sweat suit because I had to get back and forth to the doctor, and I had to wear a brace around my ribs. I had three cracked ribs, a pain in my right side that we kept praying and taking authority over, and my face was all swollen with two black eyes and a beat up nose.

I had been in the process of listening to forgiveness tapes by Kenneth Copeland that I began about three weeks before the robbery. When I had gotten on the ambulance that night, the Holy Spirit reminded me about forgiveness. So I forgave my attacker at that time as I was bleeding from my nose and face. As an act of my will, I forgave him the second I stepped into the ambulance and began praying for his salvation on the night of the robbery and several months after that. I am convinced that the enemy was not allowed to dump fear on me because I had already issued forgiveness from the time of the attack.

Even though I had forgiven him, I had some flashbacks that brought out fear that I had to take authority over. I used to sit out on the porch, which was actually a balcony of the apartment that overlooked the alleyway. The alleyway was kind of in between two houses. In Pennsylvania, they would build houses right up against each other almost making them one house. The only thing that separates them is the paint. I would have flashbacks of fear that the robber was going to come up the balcony and attack me. I just kept rebuking those fears and turning them over to God. I quoted the Word saying that God didn't give me a spirit of timidity, of cringing and fawning fear, but He gave me a spirit of power, love, and a well balanced mind with self-control and discipline (II Timothy 1:7). I'd continue by praying for this gentleman, that they would catch him, and that the strongman in his life be bound up, and that God would put laborers in his path both day and night so that he would be born again. I would start praying for his salvation in tongues and in English. I would pray this believing for I knew he needed God. Later, I had heard reports that people had gone to visit the man and preach the gospel to him.

It wasn't very long until the fears were gone. I believe it didn't take long because I forgave him the very night I was attacked. Forgiveness is extremely important to God and to us. It is important for our healing. I fought the fears with prayer, and after a short time all the fears left. I didn't have any nightmares and slept well. I used the medication to sleep only for a couple of nights. The doctors wanted me to take medications for a few weeks, which I took. But I slept a lot since it was good for my healing. I listened to a lot of ministering tapes during the day, and Bill played them all night, too. Bill called me several times a day to see how I was doing.

It was quite a lengthy ordeal. I know Bill had it tough, too. He would be gone by 7:00 AM in the morning and not get home until 9:00 PM at night, only to try to help me around and take care of me. I needed help turning over in bed, and we put a towel under me to help roll me over, but I had to wake Bill up every time to help me do anything at all. I remember once that I was stuck on the toilet. Someone finally came to the door and had to come in to help me. The pills they gave me made me have the runs. Once I couldn't get out of bed, and I messed the bed. I thought, "God, I've got to get out of this." I started crying out to God to help me. I couldn't get out, and I couldn't turn over. I flipped the blankets back, and then Barbara called me. Barbara said that Jody would come over and help me. I think Barbara must have had a key to the house. Jody came over and got me out of bed, helped me up, and helped clean me up. She changed and washed the sheets. This all happened on the third day I was home. I remember crying because I felt bad having someone else clean me up and the bed, yet I was thankful. They didn't know how badly I was hurt until then. There were several calls from the manager, district manager, employees, and police department. Jody, one of the babies in Christ from the Bible study, blessed me tremendously by helping me daily; she even recorded a song for me that meant so much. I offered to pay her, but she wouldn't accept anything. It was like Jody was born to help me during this time, and honestly I loved it. I had cared for others like this, but not many cared for me this way. Bill and I had an opportunity before to bless her by helping with her wedding and blessing her with gifts. It amazed me how it all turned around, and I was so blessed by her. She had two small children, so I know what she did for me was quite a sacrifice. She took care of me until I could get out of bed, cleaned for me, did my laundry, and ran errands for me.

Bill took me to the doctor's offices when I needed to go. For the first couple of weeks, I had to go to the doctor's office twice a week. It was all paid for by workman's compensation. I had to tell them what was going on. They put me on many different medications. I kept telling them about the sharp pain in my right side, and they kept ignoring that. So, Bill and I just prayed for healing. I slept a lot during this time. Bill would let me sleep. If I wasn't awake in the morning when he left, he'd still be sure to turn on a healing tape. The teaching/healing tapes played in our apartment day and night. We didn't need any trash or bad thoughts coming in.

There were two very good detectives assigned to the case. They came by with pictures to have me identify Richard Colefield, who they had found at the bus station drinking coffee, waiting for a bus to leave town. I don't know why they couldn't just use the surveillance tape to identify him, but they needed me to identify him. It was a while until the trial came about.

After ninety days, the District Manager of the convenience store insisted that I come back to work, even if I just sat on a stool. They would have to pay me too much money if I were to be out past ninety days. Bill was livid. I was in no way physically ready to go back to work. Bill figured that the convenient store just wanted me to quit because I would be a constant reminder to the customers about the crime rate. I knew if I quit, I'd lose everything. I, also needed the doctor's care. I asked if I could gradually go back working my way up slowly to forty hours a week. They agreed. I went in and sat on a stool making sandwiches, and I didn't have to wait on customers for a while. Bill would have to deliver me and pick me up from work. It took a couple of months until I was back to forty hours a week. During this time there were a couple of times that I fell and had to lay on the floor of the convenient store until one of the other employees working with me could help me up. Talk about embarrassing!

It was so interesting because prior to the robbery, the customers were absolutely nasty to me. Since the news reported the whole scene on all four stations around town, the customers became cool and much nicer to me. It was weird. I was even able to preach the gospel and testify to God's goodness on those news reports and a little to the customers when I went back to work.

The Lord had been working on me about impatience while I was at that convenience store. I was impatient, nasty, and disobedient to the Lord about smoking. God was faithful to work on me, especially in those three areas, while I was at the store. During the time I worked at the store, I had to learn patience. If something was my fault, they'd bawl me out for it. If it wasn't my fault, they'd bawl me out for it. I got in trouble for everything. I finally woke up and smelled the roses and realized that I needed to take it down a thousand and stop being impatient with everybody. I look at it now and know the customers and others treated me just like I treated them. You reap what you sow. Meanwhile, everyone was allowed to treat me any way they wanted to. I'll never forget it. There was a guy clear across the store at the soda fountain. There were lines at both sides of the counter. It was a busy time, and the one person that was working with me was stocking the cooler. The man at the counter was screaming at me to get him a straw. The straws were right in front of him. They weren't even two inches from his face.

I had made up my mind that I was not going to get angry. Boy, was that tough. I excused myself and went to the back, picked up the straw and said, "Here you are, sir." I gave it to him. I probably had an attitude, and he laughed at me on the way back to the counter. I didn't get angry or mouth off at him, which was a plus for me. Everybody at the counter was mad and

yelled at me. It was as though they were working together to make my life miserable.

Before the robbery, customers would call me all kinds of vile names. They'd throw their money at me. They'd continually respond to my trying to help and being kind with nasty and mean remarks. I felt more like an outsider that no one wanted. This position was very uncomfortable for me because I was still loaded with rejection. I made up my mind to be kind no matter what. There were complaints to the management as well as from the customers. I was raked over the coals about this, too. The district manager came in one day and told me and showed me how I was to treat a customer. I told her that I was treating them that way. She never believed me. The manager and district manager said that the customers continually complained about me. When I trained people, I was really impatient with them, and I needed to get over that. There was actually a whole year while I was working at the store, before the robbery, when God was really working on me. I felt like God had left me completely. I knew that I was getting a spiritual spanking. God wouldn't talk to me all year no matter how hard I begged. I can remember sitting in a chair and crying because He wouldn't talk to me. I'd pray about different things and felt like I was praying to the wall. I didn't see any answers or evidence of God in my life. Bill was working most of the time and when he was home, he was angry with me. I wasn't very nice either. I believe God was setting me free of impatience and anger. I cut the cigarette smoking down with the use of some machine, which I continually kept paying for. I just couldn't seem to quit the stupid things; I couldn't understand why.

For one full year I was being severely disciplined because of my rebellion with those cigarettes. It is far from wise to be rebellious about anything before God. One has to be willing to repent because, I tell you what, you are not going to win. I had an impatience issue, which is a pride issue. It was a hard year, but I did get set free. God is faithful.

During that time I had tried to get together for fellowship and prayer, but no one would take the time for me. I had made up my mind that I would be a good servant to the body of Jesus from that time on. That I would never let anyone go through a difficult situation by themselves as long as I have breath in my body. After the robbery, I went back to work, and I had many trials to face. We had a manager that was absolutely unreasonable. Each employee had anywhere from two to four pages listing things we were to get done while we were waiting on customers. If we didn't get them done, she would scream and holler at us about it or leave a nasty note in the book. She was born-again and Spirit-filled, but she wasn't living it. I wasn't any better. I look back now and see that we were two peas in a pod. I believe God used this manager in front of me to show me how I acted.

The manager was underhanded, game-playing, lying, etc. I asked for a particular day off, and she'd make sure that I had to work it. I remember one time that Bill and I were planning to go away for a few days. I ask if there was a good time to ask off, and she told me just put the dates that I wanted down in the book. Bill and I figured it out. As I recall, it was a fight to get the time I needed off even then. During that time, I had to go to court about the robbery. She had to know the exact time I was leaving and the exact time I was to be back. I couldn't give that information to her because I never knew. I even had to get an excuse from the court and the witness protection program each time I went, in order to be dismissed from work. There was one time in particular that I told her that I had to go to court, and I showed her the documents; she scheduled me for that same day. I told her that I was sorry, but I had to go to court. She said that I could leave from work after I came in that day. I explained that I had to go early to go to the witness protection program first, then I had to see the detective, and then go to court. She still argued with me and threatened to fire me. The district manager came in, and I told her what was going on. That made the manager mad and vengeful. She made it harder for me to go to the doctor appointments, etc. After about six months back at work, people at work began acting real funny. I had no idea what was going on. I was finally able to do all my work without help even if I still had aches and pains in my body. No one talked to me or said anything, but they were acting funny.

One day I went in and they had hired somebody from another store to be behind the counter. We then had a meeting, and I sat down on one of the milk crates that we usually sat on for meetings. The back room was open to the store on one end, so all the customers could hear if we talk-ed loud enough, and my voice does carry! There were five employees, the manager, and the district manager at this one meeting sitting in a huddle on milk crates. There was not very much room back there. The district manager started in on me and was accusing me of not liking change. I told her that I didn't object to change, and she cut me off saying, "Yes, you do hate change!" That was followed by, "I suggest you keep your mouth shut and listen." I had four other people besides the district manager bawling me out. One of them was Clara, who had asked me to come to work there to help her out. I felt betrayed. I was blamed for things I did and didn't do. I was bawled out for the way I trained people, which really wasn't my job. It was not a fair situation at all. Everyone chimed in against me, and I was totally crushed and broke down in tears.

The district manager believed that I was acting so badly because I had been beaten up and robbed. That this was the way it was at a convenient store and when an employee goes through such a situation, they need to go to counseling. So it was recommended that I should go to counseling because I was crazy. I do think they wanted me to quit because of the robbery. What a poor witness I was here!

I had to go to counseling for a certain length of time. Again, I had to get all those appointments around my schedule. But I never knew what days I would get off. The relationship with Clara fizzled out. I had prayed with her for so many things that had come to pass within the last two years. I felt so betrayed by her and a few other people that I had worked with for so long. I did a lot of work for them, which I never said anything about. It was part of that rejection again. I was really hurt by all this and have had to issue forgiveness to all involved. I put my best foot out trying to please the people, and I had strings attached to it. But that was not godly. One is supposed to put their best foot out there and give without expecting anything. I was learning that, too.

I know to this day that I got bawled out in that back office/storeroom because I was being impatient. I was walking in sin, and that was retribution for the sin of impatience. It was also a pride issue and I needed to please God, not man.

After that meeting, I still had to work that night, so I went to the list of what needed to be done that night, and I did my best without complaining. I determined not to complain even if others did. Clara knew I hated to work in the freezer, which we had to stock each shift, so she put me in the freezer. She knew I loved to do the cooler; so she never let me do it. She knew I didn't like to wait on customers, so she made me wait on customers. She did everything to be contrary. I just made up my mind that I would do my work unto God and say nothing. I even started to do extra things in the convenience store.

I did go to the counselor that the convenience store assigned to me because it was required. The district manager and manger told me that I was to go ten to fifteen times to this counselor. I had a hard time scheduling the appointments because the manager made it difficult with my times off. The counselor was nice enough but kept wondering if I still had fear from the robbery. I told her that I didn't anymore because I had turned it over to God and forgave the man. She soon realized that I had a strong belief and faith. After the fourth meeting, she reported to the convenience store that I was perfectly stable, and there was no reason for any sessions. As I remember, this made everyone angry, too. Mainly, I talked to this counselor about how everyone was treating me.

I went to work, but it was a hard place to continue to work. I remember during the time I worked at this store, there was a customer who was demon influenced. This man didn't talk at all. There were several street people who came in to buy things and urinated on the floor. Some talked gibberish, and some didn't talk at all. This particular man was obviously demonized, and he shook continually. I made up my mind that I was going to pray for him. I didn't do it out loud. I got so that I knew when he was in the area. He would sit across from the store, at the post office, and all kinds of crazy things would happen when that man was over there. I began to take authority over those spiritual forces of darkness. I prayed and declared his deliverance in every area. I'd wait on him and told the others that worked there that I wanted to wait on him. If anyone touched him, he'd freak out. I accidentally bumped him once, and he went wild. He would lay his money on the counter in a certain place and expect you to know where it was placed. He'd come in often, never speaking, rarely ever looking at anyone. If he did look at anyone, he would give an evil look. I learned how to take care of him. I would quietly anoint his stuff, plead the blood of Jesus, and quietly pray.

When I gave my two week notice for the convenient store, people became so much nicer to me. It was strange. It was like honey dripped off everyone of the customer's tongues. They all wanted me to wait on them and began being nasty to the person who I was training to take my place.

A wonderful thing did happen on the last day I was working. The demonic guy that never talked and never looked at anyone came in and bought his stuff. I waited on him, and he looked me straight in the eye, smiled, and said, "Thank you, ma'am." To me, that was the biggest thing that ever happened. Tears just rolled down my face. It was almost as if he knew that I had prayed for him. Whether he knew or not, I haven't any idea, but that was the way I chose to receive it.

Bill and I quit going to Lifeline then, and we started going to Life Center in Harrisburg. There was a lot of good things happening in the Lord there, but they wouldn't let me join in prayer because I smoked. I didn't understand at that time, but I am pretty sure that was part of the discipline from God. God wanted me to quit smoking, and I wouldn't do it. I really learned some things about the consequences of disobedience at that time.

We started going to a cell group. We got really close to the people in the cell group. Every cell group we've gone to after that one, we have never fit into. We'd try and go through the motions, but we never had intimate relationships with anybody. In the Harrisburg cell group, we established a strong bond that made a difference to Bill and me. I went to Judy and Wanda in the group and asked them to stand in agreement with me to get rid of the stupid cigarettes. I didn't want them to ask me any questions and asked if I could just report to them. That's what I did, and they prayed for a full year. I didn't feel a thing other than that God left me. It was a hard year. I look at it now and know that was a spiritual spanking because the most important thing to me was hearing God talking to me. I was around a lot of smokers and wouldn't give that up. I'd smoke about seven cigarettes a day and throw the rest out. Then I'd go right back and pick them up again. It was ridiculous.

We were still praying for a teaching job for Bill. The last year we were in Lebanon, I began to pray for Bill to get a teaching position that would fit him like a glove. I found others to stand alongside me in Harrisburg to pray in agreement. Bill and I both had a lot of refinement in those years. Bill made up his mind that he was going to start taking teaching notes and showing his faithfulness to God about having a teaching position. Bill had a great relationship with and support from the two guys named Bob in our cell group. We played miniature golf, went out to breakfast, and went to each other's houses to visit. We really had strong relationships with those people. We still have a strong relationship today. I still contact Judy on the phone, and we'll talk four to five hours. We'll just pray for one another, bless one another, and love on one another. Judy is a lady who is completely opposite of me. She is a prayer warrior, but she is a real different prayer warrior. She is anointed to give hugs. Those hugs deliver people. It is awesome; it is God.

Life Center was doing a women's retreat, so I went on my first women's retreat. I had to scrimp and save and work extra hours to afford to go, and Bill gave me some money. Bill was adamant about me going. I am not so sure that Bill did not work extra hours too, so I could go. Judy and I were all excited. It was with Diana Palmer who had been to Life Center Church. She was a prophetic psalmist. She would go around singing prophetically to people, but it was like a deliverance. You could just feel the anointing. It wasn't just a feeling; it was a knowing that deliverance was taking place. Judy and I left

Harrisburg in a car with three or four other women. The minute Judy and I set foot in our hotel room, we both started crying. We never quit. To this day, I don't know what I was crying about. Judy doesn't know what she was crying about. There were a couple of times when we boohooed back and forth and ministered to one another. How we understood each other, I don't know. We'd take tissues to the conference with us because we couldn't stop crying. We waited for a word from Diana Palmer and never got one. We sat in the meetings crying, and we'd cry all the way back to the room. The whole two days we were there, all we did was cry. When we could, I asked her, "Do you know what you're crying about?" She'd say, "No, do you know what you're crying about?" I'd say, "No." And then we'd cry some more. We came home, and I cried part of the way through Monday after we came home. Judy said, "It took my eyes two days not to be puffy from all that crying!"

The awesome thing about that whole thing was that Judy and I had a unity, a sister relationship, that I never experienced with anyone else. I know we are so different, but we love each other to the core of our beings. That lady has gone out of her way to be a blessing to me. I know that God did that through all that crying. It was a prophetic thing to put the two of us together in a room. The leaders had prayed over the rooms to make room assignments. They had ribbons in a basket that had a scripture for each person. My ribbon verse was about the mouth from Exodus 4:12. Go figure! God wanted my talking changed. God and I are still working on my speech today through Colossians 4:6. Shortly after that, Bill was offered a position in Salisbury, North Carolina.

-Chapter Eleven-

Healing and Restoration

We had more things to move this time because we had gone to a lot of auctions in Pennsylvania. We gave some of the things away before we moved to Salisbury, North Carolina.

Bill and I drove to a job interview for a teaching position. We waited a long time, and no one showed up to interview Bill. So Bill changed his clothes in the parking lot, and we were about to leave. As we were leaving, somebody came. Bill said, "I'm not changing my clothes." I said, "Fine, just go ahead and have the interview, if that's who it is. After all they are about two and a half hours late." Bill got out of the car and explained that he had just changed clothes because he thought they weren't coming. They interviewed Bill in his street clothes and hired him to teach at a middle school in Salisbury, North Carolina.

We had to go back and forth to Salisbury about three times to get Bill's medical requirements taken care of and to find an apartment. We packed and shipped our things to an apartment that we found in Salisbury. The apartment was absolutely filthy. I mean, the windows were so black you couldn't see out of them.

Our apartment in Salisbury was an absolute total disaster. When Will and I looked at the apartment and made up our minds to take it, I sat on the edge of this dusty dirty little couch that was there and cried because I didn't want to clean it. The size was nice for the price, but it was so very dirty. I refused to unpack anything until we cleaned it. I found out later that the people who lived there before us had a little pot belly pig living in the house. There was grease that was so thick on the floor in the kitchen that you could skate across it with your shoes on. It took what seemed like forever to get that stripped. The windows were black on both sides. I don't know if they had ever been cleaned. There was a window air-conditioner that was covered with dirt. Will pulled a nest or two out of it.

Will said he would help me clean it up. We took a good seven days to clean just the apartment. The three-section carport had to be emptied and cleaned.

I spent four twelve-hour days cleaning that stuff up so we could get our cars out of the yard. Once we set up our things in the large rooms, it actually was not bad.

It was a big apartment; that was a plus. We went through the same processes of being checked out as we did in Hershey. We were able to get seventy-five dollars off the first month's rent because we cleaned the apartment ourselves. This time though, we had the realty people let the delivery men into the apartment to drop off our furniture while we went hiking and camping on our vacation.

I had been sick, not uncommon for someone who had been stressed out. Stress is fear, and I felt lower than a snake's belly. God told me to watch the Rambo movies that I liked so much while I was sick. God began to actually speak to me, rather show me things about Him, while I watched the movies. In the movie, as Rambo battled his way into the Vietnam P.O.W. camp to free about ten to fifteen prisoners of war, it was as if I was in Rambo's place and it made me cry. I felt so deeply for those P.O.W.'s as they were tortured in their sewage, rat, and roach-infested cell. God then revealed to me that those prisoners were like the babies in Christ if they had stayed at that church in Lebanon, they would have died spiritually. I had a great deal of determination, like Rambo, and had ferocious determination to bring them into God's throne room and set them free. God stated that "He would never leave me or forsake me, nor forget what had been presented to these people."

The movie was such a healing thing for me as I realized that I have some "Rambo" in me, spiritually speaking, of course. He made me so that when I get something, any assignment, I won't let go.

Near the end of the rescue mission, Rambo tricks the enemy by pretending that his helicopter was shot down. Meanwhile, armed with a bazooka, he waits to totally destroy the enemy's helicopter. That is how one fights when the assignment is from the Lord. I was willing to fight to the death, but I also ended up like a one legged dog because I didn't have anyone supporting me with prayer.

Rambo called into his headquarters, where the man in charge had left him stranded, and said that he was bringing back all the P.O.W's. The man in charge of the mission resented Rambo and became angry. God showed me that there were some people in the church that would ignore me and even speak badly of me. I was instructed by the Lord to just ignore their actions, and He'd take care of it. Even after Rambo landed, he had to fight the authorities. That was the way I was with the babies in Christ. I took their walk with Christ seriously. I would encourage them and would check on them. God said that I was like Rambo, as he fought the authorities with a machete knife and blew up buildings and whole villages because when someone is trying to shut down the work of God, I get even more determined.

The third Rambo movie shows Rambo as a total outcast as he fought for the monks. God used the movie to show that I was different too, and I often felt like an outcast. Rambo's colonel wanted to send him to Russia. He did not want to go, but the colonel was captured and in trouble. He went with a rebel into the Russian Fortress to rescue the colonel. God said that I was that kind of friend and those who received my friendship would be blessed. In the process of Rambo fighting to enter into the fortress, God kept showing me that I had the bulldog tenacity and determination needed to fight the fight given to me as a Spirit-filled Christian. God also showed me that I would have friends that would fight for me the same way that I fought for them, just as the rebels stood by Rambo and the colonel to help them stay free. Near the end of the movie, there is a hole that Rambo comes out of, and he meets up with a large Russian. Rambo ignored his pain and fought the giant. God said that I would fight giants with that kind of determination and the giants would get larger, but He would show me how to fight them. God also reminded me that the battle belongs to Him, not me. I have a hard time separating that out. With each battle, I become stronger in Him because I turned my anger toward the enemy with the Word of God. So when the enemy attacks me, God actually uses it to strengthen me spiritually. So I will give the enemy a war he will not believe. To this day, God reminds me to watch the Rambo movies so He can encourage me.

I felt that I needed to go to the church where the old Bible study group was meeting in Lebanon, Pennsylvania. For some reason, probably my flesh, I felt as if I needed to check and see if they were at a good place. Why I felt that it was my responsibility, I don't know. I still deal with some of that false responsibility today that I know is not up to me.

I felt lower than a snakes' belly the day I went to visit that church. I was feeling that no one liked me, I didn't fit, etc. I thought I was the one that made all the mistakes. I was feeling down about the Bible study. I figured I had made so many mistakes that God was going to get rid of me. I felt like I had failed God. I could repent over failing people, but I just couldn't forgive myself if I had failed Him.

I went to Pastor Gibson's church that Sunday morning. I was worshiping God, and I just sat down during praise and worship with my eyes closed. I wanted so badly to hear from God. It seemed as if it had been a whole year since I had heard from Him. God told me to open my eyes and look around. Everybody else's head was bowed, and the pastor was praying. All the new believers in Christ and their friends that had been in Bible study were in this church. There were several people that were in Lifeline that were in that church. I found out that shortly after we left, Pastor Gibson had left Lifeline and felt that God was leading him to start this church.

That morning, God let me know that these people were in this church as a result of my faithfulness, diligence, and pressing in even though I had a lot of hardships and mistakes. This was a result of the prayer that I had done. I have no idea if others had prayed for these people and for this church as well. God led me to believe that Bill, my prayers, and our obedience were responsible for the raising of this church. Bill and I never said anything to Pastor Gibson. Whether the babies in Christ said anything I don't know, but I do know he treated us like we started that church, and we didn't have anything to do with it. We never helped him with it, other than we told the babies in Christ to go to a church where they would be accepted and fed the Word of God. To this day, Barbara and Chris have grown tremendously in the Lord. Barbara has been healed physically and has been delivered miraculously from a lot of different things. Chris has been delivered from smoking and other things. He has just saturated himself in the Word since we got him started. The babies in Christ that I thought would just never plug themselves in are going to Pastor Gibson's church. We've gone back to visit from time to time. More people that used to be outcasts are now attending that church. I don't know how God did it, but He did. I just praise God for it.

God had given me a vision about myself around that time. In the vision, He portrayed me as a shepherd dog that was wounded on her right side with three wounded legs that couldn't stand up. She was barely breathing. God said that this was me spiritually, that I would have given up my life for the babies in Christ. God told me that I needed healing and needed people to stand with me. I was grateful that God provided people to love me where I was in the cell group in Harrisburg. This started a healing process.

As we were in the process of moving to Salisbury, North Carolina, Bill came to me and said, "You know what, Dellana, I want to change my name from Bill to Will. I am going to Salisbury, and no one knows me there." So Bill changed his name to Will. Will did this because he had repented of a lot of different things. He had a lot of deliverances and wanted to claim his new life with a new name.

Will's new job was extremely difficult. He wanted to teach and include lab activities for the students and make learning fun. He tried so hard, but Will was up against impossible odds. His room was up against a large science storage room that he shared with another teacher. It was perfect for me to come to school and sit in this storage room while Will was having classes and pray for him and his classes. He had classes that were huge. There were anywhere from twenty to thirty students in a class. They wouldn't pay attention and wouldn't do what they needed to do. The school had metal detectors at the entrance doorway.

The requirements for teachers in this school system were unbelievable. We never got the same pay every month, so I had a hard time budgeting. Will had to attend workshops on several weekends and after school. He taught six different subjects and was required to complete the entire North Carolina curriculum. He didn't see how he could do it. He was totally overwhelmed. He got home anywhere from 3:30 - 5:00 PM, we'd have dinner, and then we'd start on schoolwork until 10:00 at night. I worked with him most of the time typing his papers. Mom Zabel had bought us an Apple computer, which was a God send.

Will's students were awful. He couldn't control them. The leadership of the school wouldn't back him up. They felt that the teachers needed to handle their own discipline. The teachers were even blamed when a couple of students were found in the bathrooms having sexual relations.

We really prayed for this school system. Not only did we pray for the system, but for the leadership of the school system and the way they set up the North Carolina law. There were a lot of politics going on. It seemed underhanded. There were numerous workshops that the teachers were required to go to and get credits that had nothing to do with teaching the students. It interfered with Will's planning time. I might be wrong, but I felt that many things were done just to look good on paper, and it broke my heart that it didn't help the students and they couldn't learn anything.

There were quite a number of teachers that they let go at the end of the year, and Will was one of them. I remember going to a board meeting after I had been involved with praying for the school for a while. The things that I heard were horrendous. The blame went from students, to leadership, to teachers, to parents, and back and forth. Everyone was just passing the buck and not doing anything about it. That was the kind of school year Will had gone through. I would say that it was the toughest year he ever had teaching. I was really glad they let him go because I felt it was a very dangerous school. We prayed for the leadership from top to bottom and saw God at work. The mighty bulldozer of God once again plowed through, and the school system is now totally revamped.

We prayed hard for the school board. There were several people let go from the board at the end of the year. There were some individuals who were caught doing some things in the school that shouldn't have been done. All of the leadership for the school was let go.

I got a job cleaning some assisted-living apartments in a huge building. They had houses, two and three bedroom apartments, and an assisted-living section as well. There was a good cleaning team there. We were all born-again except for one person. We worked together as a team. I had prayed or begged God to give me a good place to work. It turned out to be a really good year for me regarding relationships. I enjoyed the job. Compared to working at my last job in the convenience store, it was like going to heaven.

Some people were friends for a while, and some I still keep in touch with. Cedric was a joy to work with. He was a tall black man; when someone was down, he was there in their face building them up. It was as if he knew when you needed encouragement. It was so much fun to work with someone like that. Everybody there worked with everybody else. When we got done with our job, we'd help someone else finish their work. There was just real unity and a real sweet time of restoration in fellowship for me.

I had gotten down to five or six cigarettes a day. I still was beating myself up over them. There were a couple of times I'd say that I wasn't buying any, and I'd then go find butts to smoke. Some of the things we put ourselves through to get rid of addictions is absolutely nuts when God can set us free. I don't know why I wouldn't believe God could set me free from cigarettes, but I sure needed some help in that area. I needed to trust God. The Lord told me that if I was just physically dependent on the smoking, then I could quit in my own strength. Since I was not only physically, but emotionally dependent on the cigarettes, I needed God's help.

The church that Will and I went to was good. We went to the pastor's house to help him with some of his house maintenance and renovations.

They had bought a fairly old house, and he needed some help. It was nice to be able to help out. We met several people at church. We did go to some fellowships, but we couldn't go to many because school planning took a great deal of time.

There was a lady from the church that ran a laundromat. Since we didn't have a decent washer and dryer at the apartment, I went to her laundromat. She had a Pac Man video game machine there that I liked to play. She and I would minister to one another. Once in a while, there were other customers that would get in on it, too. I was able to pray while I was there. She said she noticed the difference. She had a really interesting testimony. Because of a car wreck, she had a leg that was about five inches shorter than the other one. In order to walk, she had to wear custom-made shoes. She was a really active lady and a joy to be around.

There was also a lady who I would walk down the street to once a week. We'd pray for the church and do prayer walks. Prayer was also really neat at church. Two couples would go into the prayer room and pray during the service. We would get words of wisdom or knowledge that complimented whatever Pastor Jim was preaching on. It was just God. I met and got to know Margaret who lived in the apartment across the hall from us. She had a baby, and she was a baby in Christ. Her husband wasn't saved, and he was popping drugs and drinking quite a bit. Margaret started talking about God, and I asked her if she was born again. She gave me her testimony. Apparently, she had gone to the emergency room because she overdosed on some drugs. While they were trying to revive her, she saw a vision of hell. She was just petrified and didn't want to go there. So she started crying out to God to get her out of this and promised Him that she'd give up drugs and be clean. I told her, "Someone must have really been praying for you!" Margaret had been asking God for a Christian neighbor to minister to her so she could grow in Jesus. She had been praying for her husband Tom to get saved as well. She then began to ask me questions about faith and the Word. She asked me to do a Bible study with her so she could learn. Because of school, we had to reschedule several times. Margaret rolled with the punches and was so hungry for the Word that she was a real pleasure to teach. She had so many questions. We'd pray for her husband together. We talked about the Holy Spirit, and she began to be able to use the gift of tongues. I told her several things she could do to help her husband get saved. When her husband came home totally drunk, I said, "Watch this," and I started preaching the gospel to her so he could hear it. He just sat there. I told Margaret not to worry, that I was just planting some good seeds in Tom. One time, Tom was home and wanted to ask some questions about "this God," and he was totally wasted. I just answered his questions and then preached the gospel to him. Margaret was almost doing back flips over the couch because she knew we were planting seeds. She also knew that she was to speak only positive things about her husband and not to say anything negative about him not being saved. She also took instruction on anointing her house and everything Tom owned with oil, inside and out. Tom reminded me a lot of my first husband. It reminded me to be thankful that I was no longer living in that situation. It really gave me an appreciation for Will, and I always went home to kiss my husband.

On December 31, 1999, God said to me, "Do you want the anointing or do you want these stinking cigarettes?" I said, "I want the anointing." I had prayed a lot for deliverance from cigarettes. I made an agreement between just God and me. I got up the next morning, January 1, 2000, and said that I wasn't going to smoke anymore, and I wasn't going to say anything to anybody. I said to God, "If you don't help me, I'm not going to make it." So I got up and didn't even say anything to Will.

It was so interesting because everything was funny for a full year after that. Will hardly acted up that whole year, and if he did, I just laughed. The madder Will got, the more I laughed. The more I laughed, the madder Will got. I don't even know what I thought was funny. I just know that I was full of the joy of the Lord for a whole year. I'd be driving down the road in Salisbury, and people would have their cigarettes up in the window, in the mirror, out the window, and blowing smoke. When my eyes saw what the people were doing with the cigarettes, it was a temptation to my flesh. I heard the Holy Spirit quietly on the inside of me saying, "Are you going to take authority over the enemy or not?" I didn't even know that I needed to, but I did take authority over it, and it quit happening from that day on. I sometimes do that now and pray for the deliverance of people from addictions.

About three days after I quit smoking, Will said, "You quit smoking." I said, "Yes, and I don't want to talk about it." He dropped it and didn't say anything more. Before we went to visit Will's mom, he asked me what I wanted to do about telling her that I had quit smoking. I said, "You tell her; I don't want to talk about it." I knew it could be a big ordeal. Will honored that decision. When we visited and I left the table to go to the bathroom, Mom asked about the smoking. Will said, "Yes, she's done. She quit, and she doesn't want to talk about it." Mom honored that decision and that definitely was not Mom Zabel's way.

Margaret, who lived next door to us, freaked out when Will lost his position and started applying for jobs. He applied for a job in Charlotte, North Carolina at a private school and got it. She tried to talk us out of going. I encouraged her to stay in the Word and reassured her that the lady I prayed with, who she had met before, would be available for prayer. She was concerned about Tom not being saved yet and really didn't want to let go of us. I promised to write and visit with her sometime. The last time I tried, the letter came back, and there was no answer from her. I did hear from another lady, Penny, that Tom had gotten saved. Tom and Margaret were attending church and had moved.

Will took the job at the small private school teaching learning disabled children. A small private school doesn't pay as much as a public school, but there aren't as many rules and paper work required or those silly workshops. The classes are a lot smaller too, so Will would actually be able to teach. We really prayed about taking that job. I went through the budget and books several different times. We were only paying three hundred fifty dollars for our apartment, and we knew that the rent was really high in Charlotte. Neither one of us wanted to live in a big city. We look at it now and realize that God was using Salisbury as a stepping stone because we never would consider a big city. All that traffic is stressful. I figured out the finances, and it looked totally impossible in the physical. I figured out every way I possibly could figure the finances, and there was no way it was going to work. But in the spiritual realm, of course, all things are possible.

I told Will that we couldn't pay much more rent than we were paying now. So we went everywhere apartment hunting. We saw some real dumps. One place I never will forget. I went up to the door ready to use a key to go in, but there was no door there. I walked in, and there were people there that didn't even talk to us. I walked into the bathroom, and the smell was horrendous. I don't think the thing had been flushed for a while, and it didn't seem to have much running water either. They wanted four hundred dollars for the place! We turned right around and walked back out.

We drove to Charlotte a couple of different times trying to find a place to live. I had to go to work, so Will said that he would go to Charlotte to continue the search. We had gone to Word Life Church, an awesome all black church. I told Will to go to the pastor there and have him pray with him about finding an apartment. "After he prays with you," I said, "I know you'll find an apartment, and come and get me after I get off work." Will went into Charlotte and prayed with the pastor. Two hours later, Will found an apartment for three hundred ninety-five dollars. Will put a deposit on the apartment and came back to Salisbury and picked me up after work. I sat down and tried to figure out if we could do it. It still didn't look like we were going to make it. But we had prayed about it, and we both felt like we were supposed to move to Charlotte. So we decided in faith to go and be really careful with spending our money. We went in the evening to see the apartment. It was very small with one living room and one bedroom. The rug and windows were filthy and so was the kitchen. It was another adventure in cleaning and renovating. There wasn't much carpet left, but I went ahead and shampooed it and was amazed by how much muck was cleaned up. Of course, I did this after they already "cleaned" it and after we had paid a cleaning deposit. The real estate lady we rented from in Salisbury was hard and harsh to us. She probably had a hard time with renters before, which was obvious by the apartment's condition when we moved in. I made it a point to be nice to her and to pay her the rent early. When we told her that we were moving, she actually seemed upset. A soft answer turns away wrath.

-Chapter Twelve-

The Younger Years

I had been through so many deliverances, proving that God is faithful not to keep us the way we are. So in Charlotte, North Carolina, I still found myself being worked on. I began recognizing the influences of my childhood. Growing up the way I did was not bad. It strengthened me in many ways, but there were some destructive things, too. My dad was a harsh disciplinarian. I don't remember him talking too many times in a normal voice to me; it was kind of rough and masculine. I am glad he was harsh in his discipline. I think way down deep, he was afraid that he was going to spoil me.

Dad would tell me something once and expect it to be done. I did what my dad said because the next time around it was going to be a spanking. There was no slack or grace there. Everything was pretty much black and white for Dad. If you were right, you were right, if you were wrong, you were wrong. He made it quite clear that I was going to be trained like that. He used to read the Bible to me. I don't think he ever intentionally interwove the Word with my training, but he did use some of those principles. He never really talked about God, but he spoke of what was right and what was wrong. What he wanted you to do is what was right, and when he said so, it was so. He was impatient and had a temper. He never beat me, but he sure used that razor strap on my rear end.

It was required of me to talk to my mother with respect and to follow instruction and do it right. I was to listen, understand the instructions the first time, and do it right. It was believed in my family that you don't take "no" for an answer. If you wanted something done, get in there and do it! Extreme diligence, unity, and relationship was taught, but in a harsh manner. Even if it was harsh, I respected my dad for teaching me that because it made me obedient.

Dad was emphatic about keeping one's promise. If the promise was to have lunch with someone at noon, you'd better walk through that door at 12:00; otherwise, you were a liar. He never condoned dishonesty and lying. If I ever told anyone that I would do something, even if I didn't want to do it, I would have to keep my promise. When I got out on my own, I tried getting out of my commitments, but that didn't last long. I found out that other people were not as committed to keeping their appointments, and it just made me mad. My dad used to always tell me that I was obsolete, and that there was no one else like me. He said that other people would not like me; I might as well get used to it because I was trained to be different. He said that other people just couldn't handle my honesty. I was so incredibly "honest" that I was blunt. If someone was wearing a dress that I didn't like and they asked me, I flatly told them that it was ugly. That was how I was raised.

My dad expected and required me to work hard, work fast, and learn quickly. My mother, on the other hand, was very fun loving with a simplistic nature. She took things as they came. She was very tactful, diplomatic, and accepting, totally opposite of my dad. Yet at the same time, Dad showed a lot of love and respect to my mother. Mom and Dad were both extremely sensitive. Dad would figure out quickly how people thought and would act. Mom was very good with people. She would be tactful and talk things out with people. Mom and Dad were very giving. They would put themselves out to do for others and even put off their own work to help someone else. Mom and her relatives were from Nebraska. They would write songs and play beautiful music together. Mom wrote several of her own songs that are currently in a book. She had a heart for relationships and could kindly and gracefully get the point across with her words and songs.

Mom was good at discipline, too. I had to obey her, but I could get by with doing it wrong about two or three times before I'd get it from her. Mom would usually make a joke about what someone was doing wrong. Dad would make fun of what someone was doing wrong. She was Irish, and my Dad was German. Mom was a typical soft hearted, fun-loving Irish lady who was not to be crossed. My mom was not just my mom, she was my best friend. She let me know that I was the apple of her eye. I didn't really know that Dad felt that way too until I was eighteen. He'd say things to me that indicated that he loved me, but I didn't really understand and receive that kind of love from him until I was older.

Dad and Mom, like all parents, did the best they could in raising me. There were a lot of words spoken over me that were not right, simply because Dad didn't understand the power of his words. He'd used to say, "Are you going to use your head for something else besides a hat rack?" Or "Are you ever going to be smart enough to notice?" I felt like he dumped a lot of unworthiness on me. I felt like I was too stupid and that I would never be married because I wasn't good enough for anyone. I know my dad never intended to do that.

After we moved to Charlotte, I met with my pastor and his wife to get rid of and cancel out those bad words that were spoken over and to me. I asked God if I could go through the deliverance without tears, and He allowed that. God showed me a time from my past when Dad was teaching me how to drive the tractor. I was driving the tractor crooked down the field. Dad came unglued. He screamed and hollered, threw his hat off, and told me to stop the tractor. I stopped the tractor and got off, and I was laughing. The more I laughed, the madder it made him. On the inside, I thought, "Boy, I'm glad I didn't drive that tractor right because I'd have to do all that work too!" Maybe I did that deliberately, I don't know. I could hardly push the brake and clutch on the tractor.

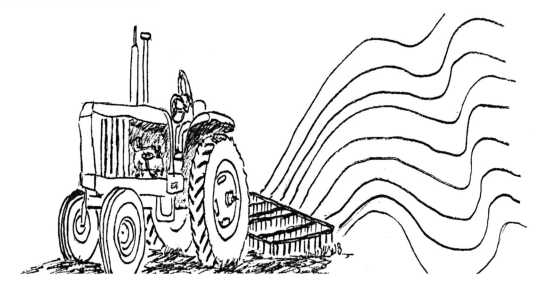

The tractor incident came to my mind as I was forgiving my dad. I forgave him for making me feel as if I was never good enough. I know that Dad never meant to do any harm to me. Instead of tears this time, I was giggling as I was forgiving him. In fact, I think Pastor and his wife started laughing with me. We began to pray in the Spirit, and I spoke out my forgiveness for certain words that Dad had spoken over me or to me as the Holy Spirit pointed them out to me. The pastor's wife felt that Pastor needed to fill in to represent my dad during this time of forgiveness. So Pastor was used by God to stand in as my father and receive the words and forgiveness and to tell me that they were received and that I was loved and appreciated. It was a major deliverance and one filled with laughter. God's deliverance can come in many different ways. It can come from learning experiences, from the Word, from someone's preaching, from the voice of a child or a person that doesn't even know God. It can be spoken, and it will click in one's spirit what God wants to bring to one's remembrance. It is so much easier to just let go and forgive someone when things are exposed that have caused pain or hurt.

When I left that time of deliverance with Pastor and his wife, I didn't feel a bit different. When I began to socialize with different people again, I realized that I was different. Something had been destroyed in me, and I felt as if I was accepted. In reality, I didn't even care if I was accepted. I was amazed. There was a Christian lady that had spoken harshly to me, causing me to go home hurt many times. This was before this deliverance. After this deliverance, I stood up to her in a nice way, but I did not put up with the harsh words that the woman spoke to me. I am still a little nervous around her, but God will deal with this, too.

Sometimes the Lord delivers us from past hurts and wrong feelings in stages or layers. About two years after the deliverance with Pastor and his wife, the Lord told me that He was going to heal me. I didn't know what I needed healing for, but I began to be very sensitive and somewhat angry with life in general. I prayed and sought the Lord as to what He wanted to heal me of. Bonnie, one of the prayer warriors at church told me that she thought it was "soul ties" that needed to be destroyed. I needed help to destroy the soul ties, which are emotional ties to someone else's personality that controlled my thoughts and beliefs. About four weeks later, I met with three people from the church for another deliverance session. I had prayed, and God had given me nineteen names of unhealthy "soul ties" that needed to be destroyed. That night we destroyed a few intergenerational things that had been in my life from birth. I felt fine when I left that Tuesday night. The next day, I was just constantly crying. I had a horrible week until Sunday. When I went back to the prayer room, the Lord revealed more about my dad. The Lord also revealed that it was not only what my dad had said to me that needed to be forgiven, but that there were also generational ties that needed to be forgiven, repented, renounced, and broken.

The Lord revealed another area with my grandma on my mom's side. Grandma would get mad at all the people that hurt her clear back to when she was a young girl. As a little girl, I thought it was funny to wait until she was really giving these people the "what for" to sneak up on her and watch her jump. I was told, "Dellana, your grandma was releasing all kinds of resentment, unforgiveness, bitterness, and fear into the air." Well, Grandma lived with us, and I received all of the above. We did the repent, renounce, break, and bless process. Again, we dealt with intergenerational issues to cover all the bases. All of the above affected my identity all of my life. Bonnie then began to bless me and fill me with the opposite good things of the Lord. Bonnie prayed for the blessings of the Lord to flow. It started as soon as I left the prayer room. It has continued each day.

I was born on November 27, 1946 in the little town of Forest Grove, Oregon. My mother got rheumatic fever when she got pregnant. When she was pregnant with me, the doctors had her down for six months due to the fever. She had a special diet and stayed at Uncle Tony's house where his wife took care of her. Mom was plunked on the couch for six months until I was born. The doctor said that there should not have been any side effects to the baby due to the rheumatic fever, but years later, I didn't have much muscle mass or energy. I had a hard time keeping up in physical education classes growing up. My legs would ache terribly, and my mom would have to rub my legs at night and put heating pads on them. When I began hiking with Will, it was really tough. That first year I went hiking with him, I didn't think I'd ever make it! When Will and I hiked, God told us to rebuke the rheumatic fever and the effects it had on me. Will and I prayed several hours on the trail over that, and we saw a miracle of God. From that time on, I began to build muscle mass. I'm still working on my arms, but my legs and buttocks have wonderful muscle mass, praise God!

When I was about two and a half years old, my mother gave birth to my sister and named her Linda Lee Fischer. My mother also had rheumatic fever while she was pregnant with Linda. She looked a lot like my dad from what mom said. Linda Lee only lived a few months. Linda died of what they called a "blue baby" at the time. Now I believe that is called "crib death" at this time. Mom was not even supposed to have any children, let alone two children. Mom and Dad loved kids, but they just could not have any more children. At the time when Linda was born, "crib death" was pretty rare and misunderstood by most. So there was a coroner's investigation because Mom and Dad were suspected of taking Linda's life. Of course, this was soon ruled out. I cannot imagine how sad this was for my parents.

Growing up, I stayed with my grandmother a lot when Dad and Mom had to go out of town. I loved my grandmother. She was my mother's mother. My grandmother and mother were simple people who loved life, but they sure could worry. Dad used to say, "Mom could worry the tires off of the car." That fear was no good for anyone, and I had to fight getting rid of that, too. There were also superstitions and silly remedies for things there were supposed to ward off evils. I'm so glad that I no longer had to drink castor oil!

-Chapter Thirteen-

The Farm

Dad had worked with his brothers in construction for many years, but his heart was in farming. Dad grew up with nine brothers and sisters on a farm, so when I was about three and a half years old, we rented a farm from an older man. He wasn't a very nice man. He had a potato farm, and I used to help pick the bugs off of the vines. I thought I was really helping him by picking off the potato bugs and putting them in a jar. I didn't trust the old man, and I didn't feel comfortable around him. I remember that he kept trying to corner me and pick me up. If I noticed that he was out in the potato field, I wouldn't go out there.

Our house had a screened-in porch, and I used to lay out there with the cats. When the sun came in, it was nice and warm. I had several naps out there with the cats piled all over me. I remember that my mom would get mad at my dad because he would go skunk hunting. Why he was going skunk hunting, I don't know! He'd come home, and he'd stink. Thank goodness I had been born without a sense of smell. Mom would make Dad change clothes on the porch, and we buried the clothes. Dad washed up some before he came in the house to take a shower.

Those are about the only things that I remember when I was that young. I don't think we stayed at that farm long because my dad had a problem with the potato farmer, too. One time the farmer picked me up in the wrong place and started moving his hand, and I thought that something was wrong with that. So I stayed away from him.

There was a gravel road going away from this farm that went across another road going to a bigger farm that my dad was interested in. Esther Stubbs, who ran the post office for Dore, North Dakota had a sister, Katherine, who owned the farm property. Katherine ran a small grocery store about a mile down the road that I enjoyed going to. Mom would give me a little money, and I could walk down and buy candy. Dad was able to lease the farm from Katherine Stubbs. The farm had a huge farm house with a large unfinished attic, a giant kitchen, and plenty of room with two bedrooms.

The farm house didn't have a bathroom when we moved in, and we used the outhouse that was about fifty yards from the house. My dad used to say to me, "Somebody will have to put bread crumbs to the outhouse to keep you from getting lost." He thought it was funny and didn't know that he was putting me down. We had toilet paper once in a while, but we mostly used the Sears and Roebuck catalogue. We got catalogues all the time.

The basement of the farm house had a cement floor where we kept our freezer, furnace, and coal bin. We used it for storage. Once in a while, Dad would have a deer down there that he had shot. Overall, this was a nice big house on a twenty acre farm. We had a small yard outside our door and an eight foot by ten foot chicken coop. We had a lot of animals including two hundred heads of sheep, a cow, forty to fifty chickens at a time, a dog, and cats. There would be more dogs when Lady had pups, and I was responsible for selling them. We sold the chickens, eggs, milk, and sheep to other farmers or traded items with them. I walked to school a half-mile. It was down by the post office. I would also walk another half a mile to the store if I wanted to buy penny candy.

The first dog we had was named Scotty. I can remember that Dad's friend came over, and I would play with his Labrador puppy. Scotty got mad, and Dad corrected him for something. I pushed Scotty away because I was playing with that Labrador, so Scotty left and we never found him. The next dog we had was part Australian Shepherd and part collie. We named her Lady. She was awesome with the sheep. Lady had a couple of litters of pups.

She had the first litter on my bed. Mom was not impressed about that because there was blood everywhere that went right down to the mattress. I was young and thought it was really funny that she had her puppies on my bed. We made some pretty good money off those puppies that time.

There are so many things that are impressionable to little children. I recall some experiences in my early childhood that left several scars on me. God has been merciful to me and has healed me of those scars. God pointed out to me that I had been rejected in the womb and told me how that rejection had happened. My dad had apparently talked to my mom about having a son while I was in her womb. I had to deal with that rejection later from the womb by forgiving my dad for wanting a boy instead of a girl.

I remember being left alone at the farmhouse at the age of four while Dad and Mom went into Fairview, Montana, which was eleven miles from the farm. I was scared and stayed on my bed with the dog for protection. When the cat jumped on the screen on the outside of the window, I thought it was a bear trying to get in. Dad and Mom, I'm sure, never knew that I was scared.

One day when I came home from school, I was playing with a plastic container that had been given as a prize at the grocery store. I broke it, and Mom asked me about it. I lied and said that, "I didn't know." Mom said, "You were the only one here, so you have to know." So I confessed. She disciplined me and sent me to my room without supper, and said, "We'll see what Dad says." Dad came home, called me out, gave me a spanking for lying, and sent me back to my room. I never lied again.

When I was six years old and living on the farm, there was a little country store about a mile from our house. I was able to go there with my allowance or reward money and buy penny candy. Sometimes Mom would give me an extra dollar if I had worked hard for her.

One day, Dad had left his pants on the floor, and I took five dollars out of his pant's pocket. When I finished helping Mom clean the house, I asked if I could go to the store. I happily walked down the road with Dad's five dollars in my pocket. Upon arriving at the country store, I bought five dollars worth of penny candy. What a sack full of candy I had! I was quite proud of myself.

The lady at the store contacted my mother and told her that I had spent a whole five dollars on candy. She thought that it was a lot for a little girl to have. She told my Mom that she thought that I had even stolen penny candy before, but she was not sure.

Well, of course, Mom questioned me when I returned home. "Where did you get the candy?" "Where did you get the money?" I finally confessed that I had taken the money out of Dad's pocket. Mom made me tell Dad what I had done. I had to apologize to Dad. I also had to take back all of the uneaten candy to the store and apologize to the shopkeeper. I had eaten about one dollar's worth of candy. I had to work and pay back the whole five dollars, plus the amount I had eaten in candy. I was given a spanking and sent to bed without supper. I never stole again because the price was too high for me!

I look back and wish Dad and Mom had taken the time to explain things to me. I walked into Mom and Dad's room one afternoon while they were being intimate. If they had explained what I innocently saw, then I would not have taken on the fear and shame I felt. They didn't know. Things were never explained and I felt frightened and ashamed about what I saw. I wish Mom would have gently explained things to me and recognized what a four year old could comprehend. I know that she tried to do this, but when I saw her change her pad in the bathroom and asked about it, she gave me full details about womanhood that confused me. I remember being scared that when it happened to me, I would place the blue strip of the pad in the wrong place. The rest of the information was forgotten about, and she told me to ask her later when I got older. But I didn't do that. Mom had been raped prior to getting married to Dad, and her mother never discussed sex, so she didn't with me either. What I learned about sex was through my Dad talking and showing me the animals and how they reproduced.

The farming life is one full of hard work. Mom taught me how to do the dishes at age four and from age five, the dishes were my chore. I showed interest in cleaning the floors, and then it was my job. At a young age, I helped to weed the garden and pick vegetables. I ate the radishes, carrots, and cucumbers right from the garden with the dirt and all. I even helped to butcher and clean the chickens. We did twenty five to thirty at a time.

Mom used to cook large meals. Dad was a big eater. She would mash up to ten pounds of potatoes for Dad for dinner. We did have leftovers from that amount, but he'd eat a good portion of it. We'd make up a lot of lunch meat to use in sandwiches during the harvest time. The families would get together and help each other harvest their farms. The women would be busy cooking continuously during harvest time. We'd drive the food out to the men and drive back with dirty dishes to clean. By the time everything was cleaned, it was time to cook dinner again. Everybody would cook in the same kitchen together. We'd have a farm harvested within two days, and then move to another farm. It took about thirty-five days until every farm was harvested. A couple of months would pass by for planting, and we'd go harvest the beans. In the fall, we harvested sugar beets. My dad designed the harvesting program so that everyone could quickly get their wheat, beans, and sugar beets out. Harvesting those sugar beets was interesting, but oh, so cold. We wore gloves to work. There was a beet topper machine that attached to the tractor. The beet topper would pull the beet up, cut the top off, and bring the beet up the conveyor belt where Mom and I would stand to pull out any extra tops and clumps of dirt. The beet would then fall into a bin where another conveyor belt would pull the beet out to where it would fall into a truck. I will never forget the day my mother tried to pull a two ton truck under the beet conveyor so that the beets would fall in. She had a hard time getting the truck straight. Dad lost his temper with Mom and got off the tractor very angry with her. Mom left the field. And, of course, since Mom left the field, I left too. So Dad didn't have any help. I heard them argue back at the house about that, and Mom just flat out told Dad that if he was going to holler and scream at her like that, she was not going to work for him. He needed to be nicer. Dad was nicer after that. He did put a lid on it, and they went back to the field to work.

Dad hated the color red. As far as Dad was concerned, red was the devil's color, and he didn't allow it in the house. So Mom and I were not allowed to wear that color. I don't know where he got that old wives' tale, but maybe he got it from his upbringing.

It was years later when I started serving God that God set me free of that superstition. God said that red and black were not the devil's colors, and that my dad's opinion was actually a lie. I forgave Dad for teaching me that. I can't tell you how much that changed me. Of course, the whole Fischer family (my dad's family) believed the superstition. I was making clothes for myself when I started serving God. I found some red and black material and made a blouse for myself. I deliberately wore it in front of my dad's family.

Dad's temper made me mad, especially when he lost his temper with my mom. I used to side with my mom during those times, but I can also remember me treating my mom badly. I sometimes acted like Mom was stupid, just as Dad had done with me. That was very wrong. I can only imagine what that must have done to my mother's emotions. I had to repent for that. It was not right, and it certainly was not honoring her. My mom deserved honoring more than Dad a lot of times. I can remember spending a lot of time by myself while I was growing up. When I wasn't going to school, I was herding sheep. I herded sheep a lot. I now look back and realize why God refers to us as sheep. The sheep would follow each other no matter what. They would never use common sense or think on their own.

We had a long grazing pasture that was surrounded by a seventy-five foot deep drain ditch and some railroad tracks that I practiced walking on. We had one lead sheep at one end of the field with me that would slowly graze down to the other end of the field, which was about two football fields away. When the lead sheep got to the other end of the field with the other sheep following her, she'd stick her head up in the air and bellow, and they would all turn around and run so fast that I couldn't keep up with them. She would come to the drain ditch, going down one side and up the other side, and crossing the road to the alfalfa field with all the other sheep following her.

Alfalfa is not good for sheep. It can kill them in a few minutes. They can't digest alfalfa, and their stomachs will literally explode. So I would run to get my dad to help get them out of the alfalfa. Dad would get a knife and needle and thread and get to the ones who had eaten some of the alfalfa. Then he would stick the sheep with a knife under their rib to reach in and take out the alfalfa and relieve the gas, while Lady and I herded the other sheep back to the field. Dad would quickly sew up the hole and move onto the next ewe. We had to move fast to save as many as we could.

Dad would bawl me out for letting the sheep into the alfalfa field. It happened about two or three times until I could convince Dad that it was the fault of this lead sheep. He finally believed me and came out to see for himself. He sat down near the bottom of the drain ditch with a two by four. The ewe went and grazed down to the other end of the field, then lifted her head and bellowed and started running. When she began to come down the

To Hippies, Bikers, and Punks With Love

left side of the ditch towards my dad, the other sheep stopped, but she kept going. Dad hit her with the two by four between the eyes. She went head over heels to the other side of the drain ditch; then she got up and tried again and got hit harder. She got up and shook her head and came at him for the third time. He hit her harder and almost killed her. Shortly after that, she was shipped to market and sold.

God has used this story several times to show me how the body of Christ is so hard to minister to. We are stubborn and want to do things our way instead of God's way. God said that the ewe was an example of how hard it is to get through to someone who is walking in pride. God wants us to repent, change our mind and our conduct, and follow Him like the sheep that followed that lead sheep that day.

One year I was able to feed three bum lambs. I spent a lot of time feeding them and taking care of them to keep them alive. As they grew up, I was able to put out grain and water for them. They were so much fun to watch as they were nursing from their bottles. They naturally wagged their tails together and when their tails were bobbed, those bobbed tails went at the same time. It was something else to watch. It was like the lambs keep time to their sucking by wagging their tails.

I traded two of those lambs for a second hand bicycle. I found out later that they were worth twenty to twenty five dollars a head. So I paid forty or fifty dollars for a second hand bicycle when I could have paid twenty dollars for a new one. My dad wouldn't let Mr. Ceder interfere with his son, Bruce Ceder, and me making a deal because he wanted us to learn a financial lesson. Dad also wanted us to learn how to make our own deals without interference from adults. It was a lot of work taking care of those sheep, so I did learn a lesson.

Lady, my dog was my best friend and later I raised a bum lamb named, Baby. Baby's face was all black and the rest of her was white. I put a bell on her, and she'd follow me everywhere. These two animals escorted me to the bus stop about a half a mile away each morning and met me at the bus stop each afternoon. It was amazing to me that these two animals could tell time! I would tell my best friends all my problems each day as they loved on me on the way to school and on the way home. I was glad to have my pets because

school was not a good time for me.

In first and second grade, I was in a little country schoolhouse that was across one of the fields. The boys would chase the girls with snakes. I put a stop to this, and everyone got mad at me. If someone new came to school, I'd make friends with them and before I knew it, they would turn on me. I never really understood why. I just felt alone, rejected, and hurt every time that this happened. I always thought that maybe I could get accepted because I stood up to these boys that were chasing the girls. That just seemed to make everyone mad. They were just playing a big game, and I didn't understand it.

In the third grade, they discontinued that country grade school. I was really sorry they did because we had a wonderful teacher. I really liked her. I actually wrote to her for years after she left. They bused us into Fairview, Montana, which was eleven miles away. It was kind of strange in Fairview. Some kids went to West Fairview, and some went to East Fairview. There was an upstairs in our school that housed the seventh and eighth grade and the boiler room. I remember going to this school in third grade, and I tried desperately to make friends with not only the country people but the city people. The city people were very different from us. What they played was not the same as our play on the farm. It was a whole new world for me. They just seemed lazy to me and did a lot of stuff that I believed should not have been done.

I remember asking Dad about these people, and I was upset about it. There was a definite difference in how they dressed, talked, and looked at other people. Once in a while, I'd have a classmate come out to the farm and stay overnight, and they'd be intrigued of how life on the farm was different than life in the city. I never understood that. They were interested in the milk cow, and I hated our milk cow. I didn't think it was easy milking that cow, and I couldn't wait to get rid of her.

I remember the city kids in school being unmercifully cruel. They made fun of my homemade clothes. They butchered my first name and my last name. They decided to play post office behind the old schoolhouse. I didn't want to get involved in that and that made me more of an outcast on the playground. If I was on the merry-go-round, they'd harass me until I got off of it. If I wanted to be on the swings, they'd harass me. My clothes even got torn a few times. Finally I decided that I would hide in the boiler room during recess time. No one ever knew I was in there until the janitor caught me and asked me what I was doing in there. I wouldn't tell him, so he took me to the principal's office. She questioned me until I told her.

The next day, all the kids had to stay in during the two recesses, and I was the only one allowed out on the playground. I thought to myself, "Oh great, now you've gotten everyone in the school in trouble. Now you're really in trouble." I didn't want the principal to do that. I didn't even want to be a part of that. It was horrible. That made the loneliness and rejection even worse. I just felt really funny about all that, even though it was their doing and not my doing. I remember after that day, things were never right. It seemed that every time a new person would come to class, I would make friends with them, and it wasn't very long until that person would totally ignore me. I suppose it had to do with the fact that I was so blunt. Also, since I felt so rejected, I am sure that I rejected others before they had a chance to hurt me again. I started keeping pretty much to myself except for the new people. But each time the new person would turn their back on me, so to speak, I became more and more withdrawn.

I remember having a third grade teacher who I really liked. I took my allowance money and bought this teacher a yardstick because she had broken hers. It was one of the good ones that was an inch thick. I was lean-ing back in my desk one day, and my teacher probably said something to me, but I didn't hear her. When I leaned over in the chair, the teacher busted the yardstick over by butt. It was the yardstick that I had bought her with my allowance! I was not impressed about that, and I felt betrayed. I felt that she had insulted her gift.

Ever since then, I had trouble with giving gifts. If the gift was not obviously accepted, I felt betrayed. God reminded me in prayer, much later in life, that I had to forgive this third grade teacher. As soon as I forgave her as an act of my will, I was free. When I gave a gift to someone from then on, it didn't bother me.

Meanwhile, I still tried to make friends at school. I had made friends with Diana, who was a Jehovah's Witness. They were very strict and didn't believe in having parties for holidays or birthdays. I hung around Diana quite a bit. She invited me to stay over at her house one night. I was in my pajamas, so I asked if it was all right if I went to the bathroom and brushed my teeth or if I need to put on my regular clothes. She said that she went to the bathroom in her pajamas all the time and that it would be all right. We had a wonderful time that night.

However, when we went back to school, she told everybody that I had run around her house naked in front of her parents. I was shocked and hurt. It gave people even more of a reason to pick on me. There were a lot of incidents like that. I hated attending birthday parties because I hated the social things. I never felt that I fit in. As a matter of fact, I felt like I could walk out, and no one would even notice that I was gone. That's the way it was for me during grade school.

During this time Baby stuck by me. Baby followed me everywhere. Whenever we needed to use her as a lead sheep, all I had to do was say, "Come on Baby, let's go," and she'd go. I remember Dad tried to get the sheep to cross the railroad tracks. Baby wouldn't cross over for him. He'd pull on her and put a rope on her, and she still wouldn't budge. He finally got me, and she instantly obeyed my voice. I began to work with Baby and Dad so that she would be a lead sheep for him, too. She was one of the best lead sheep we ever had.

One day, some man wanted to borrow Baby from me to use as his lead sheep for a while. He used her but didn't keep her warm enough and didn't take care of her, and she came home sick. I was able to nurse her back to health and spent the night in the barn with her until she was well. Then someone else came to borrow her. I even told them how to care for her and told them that if they would not follow the instructions, then they could not borrow Baby. Well, she didn't make it the second time around.

That was a real hard time. Baby's death started the cycle of sorrow and grief. I took all these things to heart. I took things literally as they were. I didn't just take it as a "part of life."

I passed all my classes even though I was so busy with trying to fit in socially. In the second part of my seventh grade year, I passed my classes on condition. Mom, Dad, and I talked about it. Dad said that I was old enough to make my own decisions. Mom suggested that I stay back, and Dad agreed. I decided to take the seventh grade over again, and I made mostly C's, but I did get some A's and B's. The second part of that year, the farm froze in. We lost the wheat, beans, and only harvested three-fourths of our beets.

Dad called it quits with the farm. They had a sale, and we owed about ten thousand dollars when we moved away from there. It was very hard for my dad. I felt badly for my dad. I am sure he felt like a failure to himself and to us.

-Chapter Fourteen-

Struggles of Life

We left our farm to go to Ephrata, Washington where Dad knew of a job helping at a farm. We arrived there only to find out that Dad wasn't needed. We stayed there for a little while, and I loved it because I didn't have to go to school. The next stop was Quincy, Washington. I was put in school there, but we only stayed a couple of weeks. I remember getting into the biology class and starting on a bug collection. I had just caught this huge Lunar Moth for the collection, and then we moved again. We went to Soap Lake, then back to Ephrata, then back to Quincy again. On the last move to Quincy, we rented a little house with two bedrooms and a bath. Dad started working with the farmers, and the checks were bouncing, which made him even more depressed. Mom was working as a waitress in two jobs. Dad overstepped his boundaries with another lady, and Mom and Dad had to deal with that. I was pretty concerned about their situation and was afraid that Mom and Dad were headed for a divorce, and I knew that I couldn't handle that. They did work it all out, and Mom was able to forgive Dad.

By this time, I was in the second part of my seventh grade year. We had moved so much, and I had missed so much of school that I was amazed that I passed and was able to go to the eighth grade. I felt kind of bad that we had to move from the farm but at the same time, I was glad that we did because I wasn't making it with those kids there. I watched some movies where one kid is treated nasty all the way through school. Well, that was me, and it wasn't funny at all. I remember the class tried to give me a party when I left that school, and I was absolutely awful. I let them have it with both barrels because of the way they had treated me. They did not act like they had any understanding of why I was acting so nasty.

We stayed in Quincy, Washington while Dad just took odd jobs and while Mom worked ten to fifteen hours a day. Grandma came to live with us. I loved my grandma. She was my mother's mother. She was fun loving and very simplistic. There was an incentive to get my homework done because then Grandma would read to me out of the Reader's Digest and books. One of the stories she read to me was "Freckles," and I just loved it. It was about

To Hippies, Bikers, and Punks With Love

a mountain girl that didn't fit in, and she went to the city. I kept thinking, "Don't go, don't go." Freckles was asked to go to the city, and I related to her so much I felt like she would not be accepted.

We thankfully still had Lady, who kept me company since I spent a lot of time alone. I graduated from the eighth grade from Quincy Middle School. I had made a point of not bothering to make friends. I just stayed away from people and every chance I could get, I played sick and stayed out of school. When I graduated from eighth grade, Mom bought a graduation outfit for me, complete with a dress, gloves, hat, and shoes. She also bought an expensive graduation gift to express how proud she was of me. I looked wonderful, and Mom and I took a picture together. We took a picture of Lady perched on a chair with her paws on the back of the chair. I carried that picture in my wallet for a long time. Actually, I still have it. My mother was very encouraging and loving toward me. She was the main person in my life that spoke positive words to me, followed by actions in everything she did with me.

Some old neighbors from the farm came up to visit us. They had relatives in Quincy and added us to their visit. I enjoyed seeing them because I had baby sat their children since I was eight years old. The three girls were like little sisters to me since I had taken care of them from the time they were newborns. The mother was concerned about the children getting away from us and running into the busy street.

Dad put Lady back to work as a sheep dog. We put Stacey, the youngest of the girls, out in the front yard with Lady. Stacey would go to the edge of the yard, and Lady would herd her back to the front of the house. When Stacey refused, Lady would gently knock her down. I watched for a long time because that was fascinating to see.

We were also near the railroad tracks in Quincy. We had bums come from the railroad tracks and knock on the door and want something to eat. Grandma used to make sandwiches for them and keep them in the refrigerator until someone came for them. She'd leave the door open and go to the refrigerator to get the sandwiches. They'd just stand there and wait for her to bring back the sandwiches. I look back and realize that bad things could have happened to my grandma, but at the time, I just thought it was normal.

Dad had gotten tired of the bad checks and Mom working so many hours that they didn't have time for one another, so Dad took a construction job in Idaho. Everything about school after that is kind of a blur to me. From the time we left from the second part of my seventh grade year until the time I graduated from high school, I had gone to seventeen different schools. How I ever graduated, I don't know. I did the same thing at all the schools I went to. I just kept to myself as much as possible and remained as unseen as possible. I didn't go to any parties or gatherings, and I absolutely hated guys. After the rape when I was eight years old, I couldn't handle the thought of being around boys.

At the beginning of my sophomore year, Dad and Mom leased the Cozy Corner Bar and store. It was a place where hunters came and rented cabins and stayed to socialize. I had a cabin all to myself with a wood stove. An old "friend" of mine from the farm, Sheila, had been writing back and forth to me. She had a lot of sexual perversion in her habits, and we had experimented "playing doctor" and exploring our bodies and other ridiculous stuff. She was a controlling, manipulative person. Anyway, Sheila had gotten a hold of my parents and asked them if she could stay with us until she finished high school. Of course, there was plenty of room in the cabin where I was. So she stayed there, and we drove this old 1949 army green panel truck that just rambled down the mountain road to meet the school bus. Sometimes I rode with Neil, Rita, Harris, and Snuffy, who were some of the neighborhood kids, down the road to meet the bus. I met Neil and Rita Bailey when they came over with their parents to the bar. Dad and Mom became friends with the Baileys who came over to play card games and to enjoy hearing Mom and me singing at the bar.

I thought Neil was good-looking, but he didn't know that I existed. Rita was sweet on Snuffy. She tried everything to get that boy's attention, but he never seemed to notice. He laughed and talked with her and what have you, but he never paid her particular attention.

Sheila came and stayed with us, and she finished her sophomore and part of her junior year. Then Buddy, Dad's old friend from the farm, came up to the bar. This man liked to wheel and deal with cars and anything else that would make him money. Sheila and Buddy got together, and she decided to take off with him. She only had one more year left of school. I thought it was stupid that she had done that, but Mom and Dad couldn't talk her into finishing school. She went off to live with Buddy.

During Christmas break, Buddy had to deliver some cars. So Buddy drove one car and towed another, while Sheila and I did the same with another car. We delivered the cars, and then we took Buddy's truck to Miles City where he had a place. Buddy and Sheila wanted to go out dancing and drinking. They asked me if I wanted to go along, and I said, "No." While they were out, Buddy and Sheila decided that I needed a man and brought a man home to me. This man was totally drunk and got into bed with me. It was awful, and I finally got away from him and told Buddy to get him away from me, or I'll call my dad. He just thought it was funny and jeered at me. So I called Dad. Dad said, "Put Buddy on the phone." When Buddy got off the phone with Dad, Buddy told the man to get away from me. The guy slept it off on the couch, and the next day they brought me home. I think they thought they were playing some funny game with me, but it wasn't funny to me.

Sheila and Buddy left after that, and I didn't hear anything more from them. He had bought her four to five hundred dollars worth of clothes in Miles City, so that she could dress the way he wanted. I saw her one time after that and she was skin and bones. Buddy was very heavy but he wanted a skinny woman. I remember Buddy was once married to my Dad's niece, then to my Dad's other niece, and then to someone else. Eventually he married Sheila. Years later when we were in Charlotte and Mom's songs were published, I sent them a copy of her songs. They emailed me, and God then had me end that relationship. God told me that I should have never had a relationship with Sheila, and that was how I had ended up in sexual perversion, and I was to discontinue the friendship with them. So I did.

-Chapter Fifteen-

Born Again in High School

While Mom and Dad were at the Kozy Korner Bar in Greenough, Montana, I went to school in Seeley Lake, Montana for my senior year. We did our grocery shopping in Missoula, our phone service was out of Ovando, we got our mail from Seeley Lake, and our electricity came from somewhere else. It was like living in 5 cities all at once. Tom Fletcher lived down the road, and he rented horses to the hunters. The hunters would rent the cabins for three to four nights. I'd build fires for them, haul wood, helped clean the cabins and fixed meals as well.

From my freshmen year until the middle of my junior year in high school, I'd ride the bus one hundred and two miles round trip to school in Missoula, Montana. It was the second longest school bus trip in the United States. The longest one was somewhere in Texas. There were a lot of times we'd have to stay home because the snow was too bad. That never broke my heart. Our bus driver used to drive sixty to eighty miles per hour, or as fast as the school bus would travel. The parents were all bent out of shape about that. If we didn't make it to school, the teachers in Missoula would give us an "F" for the day. The parents would then have to fight that. There were just a lot of politics and fighting going on between Missoula and Seeley Lake. They finally built a school in Seeley Lake. The Kozy Korner Bar was close to fifteen miles up the mountain with a curvy, narrow, gravel road leading to it.

Tom Fletcher was about quarter of a mile from the bar down the road, and he owned a business where people would hire him to be their guide and provide supplies for hunting trips to hunt deer and elk. Tom Fletcher owned a mare, named Ginger, that had lost a colt and never delivered the afterbirth; so she was all infected with scars and blisters on her backside and down her legs. I used to go after school to clean her off. Nobody else could seem to stand her stink because she was actually rotting on the outside. Mr. Fletcher had a hard time with it, so I helped with her daily cleaning and putting medication on her. He had to do it in the mornings, but I did it in the evenings and on the weekends. It hurt when Mr. Fletcher decided that she wasn't going to get well and took her to the horse dog food packing plant. He

To Hippies, Bikers, and Punks With Love

didn't tell me what he was going to do, and I thought that was pretty unfair of him not letting me know.

We used to go up to the Bailey's home a lot and visit them. There was also a man who was really into ham radios. I would often visit with him and his wife and play cards. I would also crochet with her.

When Mom went shopping in Missoula to stock the bar, she planned the trip on Saturdays so that I could go with her. People were always asking Mom to stock certain items at the bar for them to purchase from her. Mom tried to be accommodating.

During my senior year, I went to Seeley Lake High School. My parents' friends, Iola and Ben, used to come up to the Kozy Korner Bar and played and sang. Ben was talented with the guitar and other instruments. Whenever they would come up on Friday and Saturday night, I'd stay with their five children. I would just come from school Friday night and stay at their home until Sunday. In order to have me at Seeley Lake High School, Mom and Dad would have to get up early every morning and drive me to school. It was difficult because the bar would sometimes stay open after 2:00 AM, if there was a party. So Iola, Ben, Mom, and Dad made a deal that I would stay with Ben and Iola and get up with their kids and go to school because they lived closer to the school. That way they would have someone for a baby sitter on the weekends. But the pay ended then for the weekends of baby sitting.

Well, I am a worker. That was the way I was brought up. Iola was smart and fun to be around, but she was pretty lazy. All she wanted to do was to sit in a chair and read a book. The children, Gary, Sally, Joe, and David helped me take care of Violet, the newborn. The kids would take turns doing dishes, and I would have to work with them for most of the night to get the dishes done. Sally's bedroom was absolutely atrocious. She couldn't find the floor or the bed; so I'd clean that up.

Ben used to fuss at Iola about not getting up with him. She'd listen but wouldn't do anything about it. They loved one another but had some real arguments. It ended up that the more I did, the more they expected. I got up early in the morning. Ben had to be at work at 5:00 AM. I'd feed him breakfast and fix a lunch for him to take. Then I would fix all the kids breakfast and lunches. I'd take care of Violet, change her, and get her ready for the day. After school, I'd clean the house. It wasn't a very big house, but it still took time, especially cleaning the breakfast dishes that had food on them all day long. It took so long to get the kids to do the dishes that most of the time, I just did them myself. Generally, I would go home on the weekends after that. Mom and Dad would come pick me up, and Ben and Iola would hire someone to baby-sit their kids when they went to the bar.

Iola and I did get along and had a good time. In fact, she was the reason that I made it through English. She would help me write my papers. Then she would rewrite them, and I'd copy it and hand it in. Iola and the kids went to the Baptist church in Seeley Lake. They got me going, too. All they ever preached was salvation. If you went to that church, you'd better get saved. I did get saved when I was around fifteen or sixteen years old, which was around 1962 or 1963. In fact, I got saved more than once.

They had a youth group on Sunday night, and Raymond led that youth group. He was six foot two inches, and he was handsome. I was stuck on him, and he didn't know I existed. His younger brother wasn't too bad looking either. They had seven kids in that family and when the father died, the mother did a great job raising all those kids. I went to their house a few times to help with a few things. I don't really remember what I did, but I'm sure it was just to be around those two boys. Raymond made school a little easier because he traveled the one hundred sixty mile bus trip too and was very kind.

I ranted and raved to Dad about the pastor and his wife. They wanted a baby. I prayed that they would be able to have a baby, and they did finally get to adopt a little girl. I would ask the pastor all kinds of questions about the Bible. I asked mainly about why God didn't talk to us. He never really answered me. I don't think he knew. I made a point to go to youth group regularly, but that was just so that I could be around Raymond. We had hay rides and had some fun activities. Of course that church said, "Don't dance, don't smoke, don't drink, don't go into a bar, wear your dresses a certain length, don't wear make-up, etc." They taught a whole bunch of rules. I often wondered, "How will these people ever get saved if I do not go into the bar and tell them about Jesus?" I thought these people certainly are not going to come to the Baptist church to get saved!

My dad wanted me to learn to dance, and I had trouble with it at that time. I wouldn't go into the bar. But I had to go in and help in the store. I did help Mom cook Chinese fried rice and help out in other ways. There began to be weekends that I wanted to go home, but Iola said, "No, you have to stay here." Dad finally asked me about it. I told him about getting up in the morning at 4:00 A.M. and fixing breakfasts and lunches and trying to stay awake for my classes. I told Dad about cleaning the house and the one child that walked in his sleep. He would get up in the middle of the night, sleepwalking, and pee in one of the other kid's shoes. I cleaned that up and changed their beds. After I told Dad all that, he didn't say anything, but I knew he was mad. He had a chat with Ben and Iola, and I was pulled out of the house.

For the last of my senior year, I stayed with a girl whose family had just moved to Seeley Lake. I'm not sure what happened there. I think they had gotten another job and had to move. This home was less than three miles to school. The rule was that if the house is less than three miles to school, the students had to walk. We were also required to wear dresses. It was below zero one day and snowing, and we were walking to school. My legs below my knees to my ankles were freezing. On the way to school, the principal stopped and asked why we were walking. We told him that we lived less than three miles away. He said, "Ok, then," and he left us to walk. When I arrived at school, my legs were frostbitten. My math teacher noticed the welts on my legs, and my legs felt as if they were on fire, and they itched. The math teacher sent me to the women's rest room and told me to keep pouring warm water over my legs. Then he said that I was to report back to him in an hour. I did what he told me to do. After an hour, I went back to my math teacher. He took me to the principal to have him take a look. Two or three other teachers looked at it and went off and talked by themselves. Then they came back to talk to me, and they called my parents. I went home and soaked more in warm water. I was thankful that my teacher had caught it in time and gave me good instructions.

Then I stayed with a girl who was a sophomore at Seeley Lake. I had stayed at three different places during my senior year, but at least I was able to stay in the same school. I was pretty proud about being one of the first students to graduate from that school.

I remember we used to get so excited when the show "Secret Agent Man" came on the television. We both really liked that show. I think we liked the music more than anything else. We'd hurry and get our homework done, have our dinner, and watch "Secret Agent Man" on Wednesday nights.

I graduated from Seeley Lake and wore an outfit that my sewing teacher had made me change. I had made a dress and jacket, and I had designed my own and made it reversible. That was my senior project. The pattern did not call for it to be reversible, nor did it tell me how to do it that way. I had it all done, ready for graduation, and the teacher told me to change it back to what the pattern said or else she would flunk me. She told me that it was quality work, but that I had to follow the pattern. So I had to tear all of that out and make it out of a blue and black brocade fabric. I was so upset. I wore the dress and jacket for graduation and just gave it away because I would never wear it again. I wanted it reversible.

When I began sewing again, I had a lot of difficulties. Everything I attempted didn't work out. The Holy Spirit brought back to my mind the problems I had with my graduation dress and jacket. God told me to forgive my sewing instructor, and I did. After that, the Holy Spirit began to help me learn to sew all over again. You see, it had been years after graduation that I had even attempted to sew, and it was because of that teacher and the dress and jacket incident. I can remember several occasions when I didn't know how to do what the pattern was saying, but the Holy Spirit would give me a picture of it, and I'd know how to do it. On some of those occasions, I could go to town to a sewing store where someone would help me as well. We are born with particular gifting, and the Holy Spirit teaches us to use those giftings throughout our lifetime, whether we're born again or not. But it is best when we are born again and Spirit-filled because we are more in tune to receive direction from the Holy Spirit for our good and for God's glory.

-Chapter Sixteen-

Naive at Eighteen

After graduating from high school in 1965, Mom, Dad, and I headed out to Salem, Oregon for a vacation. We visited some relatives out that way and stayed at Dad's oldest brother's house for several nights. They asked me to stay for the summer to house sit while they went to Europe. They had a huge house with four bedrooms, including a huge master bedroom with a giant bathroom to go with it. It took two or three days to clean the house and weed the front and back yards. I was not used to such a big house, so once I cleaned a room, I shut the door and operated out of one room. I brought in the newspapers, mail, and took general care of the house while they were away.

My cousin, Shannon, had dated a boy named Bill Pearcy once in a while. I met Bill, and we started dating as soon as Shannon left for Europe. You would have thought I would have got the picture about Bill's character then. We went to the drive-in movies a lot. He had a motorcycle. We went everywhere on the BSA motorcycle that didn't have a buddy seat. I remember rolling up a towel and tying it to the fender, and I used that as my seat. I didn't know that I shouldn't wear shorts on the bike, so I faced the result of burnt legs and have the scars to prove it. I soon learned to wear long pants no matter how warm it was outside.

We took the BSA to the ocean several different times. I was intrigued with the ocean because I never had been around the ocean before. Something about the ocean attracted me to it. I remember thinking and saying, "How can anyone not believe there is a God?"

Once in a while we went to Bill's mom's house. It was a rundown two bedroom house that had a tin roofed carport attached to it where Dad Pearcy parked his car. Up a ways from that, Bill had a shop where he worked on motorcycles and antique cars and bikes. For the most part, when we dated we went to the movies, rode around on the bike, or went to the ocean. We saw each other almost every night until my aunt and uncle got back from Europe.

My uncle was extremely bent out of shape when he found out that I was dating Bill. He laid into me, and I was not used to that. It upset me so badly that I called Dad and told him that I needed to come home. My uncle wanted to pay for the bus ticket, but I insisted that I would clean the houses that he built and work for the money instead. When I had earned enough, then I would go home.

Shannon and I were working three to four days a week cleaning houses. I was eighteen, and I was convinced by the enemy that I would never get married because I was not good enough for anyone. Bill treated me well, and he wasn't pushy with me, so I'd sneak out the window to go see Bill while I was earning money to go home. We'd sit in the car and talk. We were both bent out of shape about my uncle's reaction to us dating. My dad had talked to my uncle about us, and it made the situation worse. If my uncle would have just left it alone, I probably would have made the decision on my own not to marry Bill. Marriage probably would not have come up because I do not think Bill was really ready or wanting to marry anyone at that time. Since the issue was pushed, and I told Bill about it, Bill suggested that we just go ahead and get married. I said OK. I was young and naive. The whole thing just got more exciting the more we snuck around. I had no idea what I was getting myself into. If I'd known, I probably would never have married the man. Although, I'm not sure. I was so full of rejection, unworthiness, loneliness, shame, guilt, and God knows what else. Who knows? I did earn enough money for the bus ticket and went back to Helena, Montana to see Mom and Dad. I told them about Bill, and that he wanted to get married, and that I had said yes. I know Dad talked to his brothers about it, but I don't know the details of the conversations.

I had asked Bill to come and ask for my hand in marriage. I just thought that it was the right thing to do. Remember, I was born again, but I was not living for God. I do not know what I would have said or done if Dad had said no. In about three weeks, Bill fired up an old car and came to see my dad. Mom and I left the house while Bill talked to my dad. He did ask for my hand in marriage, and Dad gave him fifty dollars and an old Chevrolet car with his approval for us to get married.

On our way from Montana to Oregon, a rod busted in the car's engine. We stopped in a farming area and were given permission from the farmer to park in the back of his property while Bill tried to fix the car. Bill thought that he could work the car on five cylinders instead of six. It never did run. So we called my parents, and they came and got us. We had that car towed away. Mom and Dad drove us to Salem, Oregon. When we got there, we told Dad's youngest brother and his wife that we were getting married. We told the oldest brother that we were getting married. They changed their tune. No one wanted me to marry Bill, but Dad and Mom never said a word. I know deep down in their hearts that they didn't want me to marry this guy either, but I had to make my own choices.

Bill and I grabbed some donuts, and we went to visit Tom to ask him to be the best man. For some reason, I fell asleep on the couch. I woke up from a nightmare, screaming and crying. I didn't want Bill to touch me, but he kept asking me what the matter was. When I finally woke up, I told Bill and his friend about the rape. That was the first time I had ever told anyone about the rape from when I was eight years old. It dawned on me that I was going to get married, and sex was going to be involved. I was so very scared. Bill was very compassionate and understanding about it. He never pushed me into anything, and I appreciated and respected his kindness. We didn't have a lot of money. Dad's youngest brother's wife helped pay for the wedding dress, so I got to pick out a dress that I liked, and I tried to keep the price of it down. The oldest brother's wife had a reception at her house for us. Some of Bill's friends came to the wedding. We got married in early October 1965. It wasn't a very big wedding, just twenty people or so. I don't recall where we went on our honeymoon. We just went to the ocean over night. Bill then took me back to his mom's house, and we stayed in his bedroom. After we were married, I was still concerned about sex. Bill never pushed me; he never pushed me about seeing my body or anything like that. He just waited for me to come to him. I really do not think Bill knew any more than I did about sex. On our wedding night, we tried to do what married people do without success, so we got up in the middle of the night and ate pickles, ice cream, and wedding cake. We didn't even consummate the marriage because of my problems. One of the reasons why I fell in love with him was probably because he never pushed me in that area. It probably was a good three weeks until he ever saw my body.

Mom and Dad Pearcy were angry that we were staying in their house and eating their food. They wanted us out. I am sure that Dad Pearcy wanted us out because he was an alcoholic and the cost of us being in their house would take money away from money spent on alcohol. Dad Pearcy was the kind of alcoholic that would be sober for several months, and then all of a sudden for no apparent reason, Dad Pearcy would get drunk and stay drunk for three to five months or more. We would have to steal his car keys or dismantle his car to keep him from driving or getting hurt. Mom Pearcy acted like she was ashamed of Bill. It was just a mess.

Grandpa Pearcy had a shed about four blocks away from Mom and Dad Pearcy's house. It was a long shed that they had kept cans and plants in for Knight Pearcy Nursery. The land was all Grandpa Pearcy's. Dad Pearcy worked for Grandpa Pearcy, and their house was built on a portion of Knight Pearcy's Nursery. The long shed building was ours to live in if we cleaned it up, and he had us work at the nursery. The shed had about five inches of thick mud dried onto the wooden floor, but it had a little stove in it. For about a week straight, I went up to the shed, took a scoop shovel, and cleaned out the mud and the cans that were stacked clear up to the ceiling. Bill helped do some of it, but for the most part, I did it. We took Bill's single bed and started creating a home. We eventually got a double bed, and I made a curtain from an old sheet to create a separate room. We kept the single bed as a couch. We also found an old table. Someone gave us an old carpet that I used by the single bed. I set up the electric frying pan, which was a wedding present, and I cooked everything in that, including bread.

We didn't have a refrigerator or a place to plug one in, so we took a can that I had gotten from cleaning the shed, found a large board to go over the can as a lid, and a couple of large rocks to hold the lid on the can; this was our refrigerator. We had quite a few wild animals that would enter the shed, so we had to secure our food tightly. Mom Pearcy would let us use her refrigerator and freezer. I hated having to walk back and forth to get the food. I hated walking through those trees because it would remind me of the time I was raped. I was absolutely petrified walking those four blocks through the trees in the day time, so I rarely walked up there in the dark. I remember begging Bill to go with me if I went at night or asking him to go instead of me.

Grandpa Pearcy hired both of us to work in the nursery. It was kind of fun rooting and potting the plants. All day long, I would take a little plant, stick it in some white fertilizer, and then put the plant in a small planter with some good dirt. Bill worked with the bigger trees. It was minimum wage, but it was a good job. I was under the impression at that time that the man of the house should be in charge of the money, so I would always give Bill my check. We were paid weekly and went to the grocery store after payday. Then Bill would go buy car and bike parts. My bras had worn out, so I asked Bill if I could have some money to go buy new bras. He wouldn't give me any money. Bill wanted to keep the money that he earned for bike and car parts. I realized he was pretty selfish, so I decided to keep my own checks from then on. Meanwhile, I wore out the last bra. I wrote my mom, and she sent me ten dollars for three bras.

For fun, we still went to the beach or to the drive in. Once, Mom Pearcy invited me to a Tupperware party at her house with her friends. I put on a dress, and she gave me a pair of nylons to wear. I was right in the middle of the Tupperware party and having a pretty good time. I had done all my housework and was off that day, so I didn't see a problem. Bill came up there and just had a fit; he jerked me out of the chair, ripped the nylons off me, and told me that I'd never go to a Tupperware party again. This was in front of Mom Pearcy and her friends. Talk about embarrassing! I didn't understand what the problem was. He just screamed at me all the way back to the house. We had a rip-snortin' fight. I think that was the first time that he hit me and called me names. I left for a while and then went back to him before dark, but I didn't talk to him for three days. It cooled down, and I just decided that I wouldn't go to any more parties. I never did understand Bill's thinking about this, but I think he was afraid I would be like his mom. He acted like he hated her at times.

Once in a while, we'd get donuts and go to Tom's to play games and visit. Tom was a pretty cool guy. He had some emotional hang-ups but was really fun to talk to. Bill met and befriended a whole bunch of people. We visited a lot of people that were into car repairs and had a lot of car and bike parts. We often went to the junkyards to find parts.

One night we were sound asleep, and I had a dream that Tom had a gun to his head and was going to kill himself. I woke up in a cold sweat and started getting dressed, waking Bill up at the same time. I told him we had to go to Tom's. In the process of him getting dressed, I told Bill about my dream.

When we got to Tom's house, we knocked on the door. There was no answer, so we just went in. Tom had a gun in his lap ready to kill himself. Bill and I started talking to him. Bill finally stepped to the side and just let me talk. Tom listened to me and gave the gun to Bill. We stayed and talked more for a few hours until we were sure that he was all right. Anytime after that, Tom would call us if he needed someone to talk to.

Mom Pearcy began to allow me to do some baking at her house. Baking in the electric skillet was not very successful. Bill was critical about my layer cakes, and he wanted his layer cake perfectly straight. I tried hard to please him. One day I made a beautiful layer cake that was perfectly straight and was so proud. I made a fancy meal that night with all his favorites: steak, baked potatoes, clam chowder, and string beans. I was all dressed up and ready to enjoy the romantic evening. When Bill came home, he had spent most of the money we had on car parts, and I confronted him about it. The fight was on. We started screaming and yelling at one another and calling one another terrible names I never heard before. The next thing I knew, to get even with me for the confrontation, Bill took the bowl of clam chowder in the palm of his hand, lifted it high, and turn it upside down in the middle of the layer cake. He went screaming out of the house and up to his shop. I felt insulted, rejected, and didn't want to forgive him for that.

Another time, someone from Arizona came to visit us in this shed. Chester had no place to stay, so Bill and I had him stay with us. Chester was very strange. He did not want to cook, but while I was cooking he would tell me how to do the cooking. If I was cooking hamburgers, Chester would have to stand as close as possible to tell me when to turn each hamburger, always letting me know that I did not know what I was doing. Chester made fun of me a lot as well. When I told Bill, he simply laughed about it. When Chester helped me turn hamburgers, I finally got angry and slapped him with the pancake turner. It made no difference. Chester would get up in the late morning and stay up late at night. He just walked in our bedroom whenever he felt like it without knocking. Chester was very annoying all the way around. He would not listen to anything you would tell him. Finally, since Bill was not going to do anything, I told Chester to get out in two weeks, or I would throw his stuff in the muddy yard. I helped Chester try to find an apartment. There was always something wrong with it. I told him, "You are living in a two room shed now and seem to think it is ok, and that is because the price is right."

Finally, the end of the two weeks came. Chester had not moved. I did just what I said I would do. Chester came home and said nothing. He slept in his car for a few days. I guess he thought I would change my mind. I stood my ground. Chester finally went back to Arizona. Bill then told me that Chester went around the country wearing out his welcome everywhere he went.

We went to Chester's house in Arizona once. Man, was that a trip. Chester had a sister and his parents. They did not talk much to one another other than to fight. The four of them were constantly putting one another down. We only stayed one night and day. I insisted that we leave. Why Bill listened to me, I will never know, but he did.

We also met a lot of hippies. They were kind of cool people and fun to be around. I began to collect yarn at Goodwill stores, and people would give me yarn as well. Since I had learned how to crochet from my grandmother when I was nine years old, I put that knowledge to work and made a lot of Afghans. I got a lot of attention making Afghans, and I would make and give one to whomever because I wanted to belong.

We were married about eight months when Bill got drafted into the Army in May of 1966. Bill drove me in an old Studebaker that had no muffler or a hood and took me back to my mom and dad's to stay and work while he was in the service. It was in the middle of the winter, and we went from Oregon to Montana in the Studebaker. I got very sick with a headache and puked my guts out from the fumes of the exhaust. We stayed overnight at a hotel where my headache went away. I finally felt like eating some soup. But as soon as we got in the car again, I was just as sick.

We finally got to Montana, and it took me a few days to heal. Bill took the bus out of Missoula, Montana to boot camp and left me with that faded red/silver Studebaker. I didn't know how to drive yet, but I tried to learn on that thing. I used to drive it to the store with fire shooting out of the carburetor while I passed policemen on the road. The policemen would never stop me; they would just shake their heads. I was amazed. Do you know how much trouble I would have been in? I had to park this car on a hill so that I could get it started again. I don't know how many times I got stranded in the parking lot and had to get help.

My dad and I finally went to my uncles. He worked on cars, and he was good at it. He had a Rambler that was in pretty good shape. It had a shift on the column, and he told me how to use it. He warned me to be careful with it because it could easily get stuck in gear. So I spent fifty dollars and bought the car. Mom would have me drive with my learner's permit to our cleaning jobs until I was ready for my license. I found a little eight foot by forty-five foot Streamline trailer house. There was a trailer lot available at that same time. I had to have Dad sign for me, but I was able to get the trailer and put it on a lot, not too far from my parents' trailer. It was an old trailer. I cleaned it up, insulated the pipes, and skirted the bottom of the trailer well. I didn't have any money to remodel it, but I found a couch and various items at Goodwill and garage sales. Bill's Studebaker that had no hood sat in front of the trailer. I covered the car with a blue tarp and tied it down to protect the car from the snow. I went back and forth with the little Rambler for a while. I got it stuck in gear and got it out a few times. One time I got it stuck, and it just stuck in second gear. I finally drove it to my dad's brother-in-law's place and just left it there. Dad and I came home and I bought a little Dodge Lancer. So while Bill was in Vietnam for eighteen months, I bought two cars and a trailer house, paid for all of them, and was in a bowling league with 148 point average.

At the end of twelve months, Bill wrote to me and said that he was going to be in Hawaii, and he wanted me to fly over and meet him there. So I made arrangements to go. About two weeks before I was scheduled to leave, Bill wrote me a letter and told me not to come to see him. He said that he couldn't stand me being in Hawaii for seven days with him, and he'd just go by himself and get himself a hooker. I just went ballistic after reading that letter. I just lost it. I could not believe he would do such a thing, and I decided to start partying.

I ran into this nineteen year old girl who was staying with her aunt and uncle in the trailer court. She gave me the sob story that they wouldn't let her stay out at night and wouldn't let her go partying or date. So I offered her an opportunity to be my roommate. She paid me for the first few months, and then she stopped. She began using her money to do other things, and it became a zoo of guys running in and out of the trailer.

The day I got the letter from Bill about him getting a hooker in Hawaii, she and I went out. We met four guys at the drag strip, and I just got plastered. I don't remember what happened, but I was told that I was a mess. They were supposed to have taken us sledding the next day, and I woke up on the couch just sick. She wasn't feeling too good either. These guys were supposed to pick us up, and we discovered that these guys had stolen a bunch of stuff out of the trailer. After I healed up, I told her that I couldn't have her going out for two to three nights without me knowing where she was in case of an emergency. I finally got through to her, and I know I wasn't a real nice individual at that time. The more hurt you get, the harder you get.

After about two months, she moved out and owed me rent money for several months that I never got. I decided that I was not going to rent to anyone else again. I stayed by myself. Dad had a job doing construction in Idaho, and Mom went with him. On Fridays, I'd find someone to go party with, or I'd go party by myself. There were two single guys in the trailer next door to the landlords after Mom and Dad moved. One of the guys, John, was pretty good-looking. We went out a couple of times. I ended up in bed with him. They invited me over to their house for a party. I don't know what attracted me to John because it was awful with him. I suppose I used him to get even with Bill, and all it did was make it worse. John was also good in helping me with my trailer with frozen pipes, skirting, and anything else that needed fixing. I finally broke it off with him, even though he lived next door to me. He would continue to come over and try to push his way in, but I said, "No!"

I pretty much stayed by myself and started just keeping busy with work. I was tired of just going to the bar and playing name, rank, serial number, and "let's go to bed." It was so ridiculous. I just stayed busy doing odd jobs and crocheting. I baby-sat on the weekends and cleaned during the week. So I stayed busy enough to be too tired to party.

When Mom and Dad would visit, I would go have a few drinks with them. One day, Bill got out of the service. He didn't call me or anything. He just came to Missoula and showed up one early afternoon. When he knocked on the door and I opened it, I ran the other way. I was so shocked to see him. Of course, I went back and greeted him. I guess somehow I thought it was over because of the hooker in Hawaii. Bill showed me all the pictures he had, and he brought home a picture of the hooker that he had seen in Hawaii and all that they did. I thought that was real ugly. It was just hurtful. I asked him, "How could you do that? How can you bring that home and rub my nose in it?" He just laughed. He just didn't have any respect for females at all. We then had to talk about what we were going to do next. Bill was tired, so he went to sleep. I was working around the house when I heard a real loud noise that sounded like a sonic boom. I went into the middle bedroom where Bill was sleeping, and he was on the floor trying to crawl underneath the bed. In a trailer house, you can't do that because the beds are like bunk beds with drawers underneath. So I woke him up and got him back into bed. He slept for about twelve hours.

We took Bill's car back to Salem. Then we borrowed a truck and came back to pull the trailer house. Bill wasn't too good about cleaning the trailer house or cleaning up the area from the skirting and insulation. We had trouble hooking up the trailer with the lights, etc. I never admitted it, but Bill was really not a very good mechanic either.

I followed in the car behind Bill who towed the trailer. We had to stop at every weigh station. We stopped at the first weigh station, and the turn signals, brake lights, parking lights, and other required lights weren't operational. We had to stay at the weigh station until they were fixed. It wasn't really cold out, so that was a plus. We slept in the trailer house at the weigh station while Bill tried to fix everything. He wouldn't ask anybody to help him because he was a mechanic. Bill never liked a lot of hassle either, and he was having a fit. He was also not very responsible and was definitely against any rules that anyone laid down for anything. We finally got all the lights fixed and made it through several weigh stations. We did have to stop at one weigh station because we didn't have a permit for something. We took care of it. Thank God it didn't take any money because we didn't have a lot of money.

It took about five days to get to Oregon. My dad's older brother said that we could live on his property and not pay any rent. He had about twenty acres, and he could put us clear in the back at the bottom of the hill. He helped us set up. Bill had to help with that, and he didn't like doing that either. What my uncle required from Bill was help with any mechanical needs around the house, and he was supposed to rebuild a truck that my uncle had. I was supposed to weed the garden and all the foliage in front and back of their house and clean their huge house, too.

Bill and I had taken some time after we had set up the trailer to go to California on a vacation to our aunts. I guess we were gone about three weeks. We visited Bill's aunt on his mom's side and my aunt. We went to Disneyland for a day. Bill's aunt had a pet monkey that was kind of fun but very dirty. I found out on this trip that Bill had gotten into smoking pot, better known as marijuana.

-Chapter Seventeen-

Hard Labor

Bill did work off and on. He spent most of his money on bike parts and would buy groceries each week. It probably would have been better for us to pay forty-five or fifty dollars a month to rent a trailer space for our trailer than what we were working for at my uncle's house. Bill didn't like to work and wouldn't work. I went to work at one cannery and then took a second job at another cannery. It took Bill quite a while to rebuild the truck for my uncle. Bill would also ride the mower to cut my uncle's yard. I worked the cannery jobs and spent whatever time I had off working for my aunt. She was quite a difficult woman to work for. After a while, my house was a mess with dishes just stacked in the sink. I tried just leaving the dishes in the sink until Bill would wash them. It didn't work, and I finally had to wash the dishes that were stacked almost clear to the ceiling.

My hours at the cannery increased from twelve to sixteen hours a day, and my aunt still expected me to clean her house, take care of her gardens, my house, and cook our meals. It was hard for me with no help from Bill. It caused quite a conflict between Bill, me, my aunt, and my uncle. Bill spent his time getting bike parts and traveled twenty five miles to and from the shop next to his parents' house where he spent most of his day. Bill didn't like the trailer; it was too small and too much responsibility, so we sold it. We rented an apartment for a short time.

He bought one pair of pants, and he didn't want them washed. These pants were called "slicks." I did not know he was making slicks so I washed the pants. He beat me up over it and almost broke my big toe and bounced my head on the cement floor of the apartment. I moved out for awhile and I moved back again. That was pretty much what our lives were like. That was the time we hung around some hippies and bikers. We hung out at their houses, better known as pads, where we had parties and experimented with drugs.

Once in a while we went to the ocean or to the movies. Mostly we went to visit people at their houses. That was when I met Bob and Fran. They were hippies, and Bob was called Suzuki Bob. We hung out with the twins, Mouse and Beanie, who were really fun girls, all of four feet and five inches tall. We went to one party at Mouse and Beanie's. I sat next to this dark haired chick, and all of a sudden, I began to share her whole life story, where she was going, and what she was going to do. That's when everyone made a big deal out of it and told me that I had ESP. I felt really important.

We began renting a basement apartment. I cut back to working at only one cannery. I got tired of picking beans. As a matter of fact, I got motion sickness working there. I kind of enjoyed working at the pear factory. I would put six pears in a machine that peeled, sliced, and cored the pears and sent them on a belt with the sliced pears. Then the women at the next station would cut any damaged pieces out of the sliced pears. Believe it or not, the garbage off the floor is the baby food. I thought if I ever had any kids, I'd never feed them that. In fact, it has taken me a long time to eat pears again.

I could tell that Bill was involved in something. He was always short tempered, but sometimes he was really energetic and then had no energy at all. We saw more of Bob and Fran and began smoking pot. We had quite a few parties at Bob and Fran's. Of course there was alcohol there; there were also Dextrine and Benzedrine (which are uppers). We started off with Benzedrine and pot and hash. I really didn't like the hash or marijuana, but I really like the Benny's. I actually made the decision not to take them again because I did not want to get hooked on any drugs.

One night, there was a party at Bob and Fran's, and there were bikers there. One biker was really big and muscular, with a six foot two frame that filled the doorway. He kept bothering me and trying to get me to have sex with him. I told him to get away from me, that I was married and not interested. He still wouldn't leave me alone. I finally went and told Bill about it and he said, "You're going to have to stand up for yourself!" I don't remember exactly what I did. I stood up and got really angry and screamed in his face quite a few profanities. Then I ducked under his arm and went to the other side of the room. This big red-haired bully just sat in the corner and whined because I wouldn't do what he wanted. Bill thought it was really funny. I didn't know that I was opening a door for anger to take root. I became much angrier after that.

Then Groggy, another guy like Bill, began making passes at me. But I knew Groggy was just kidding because he always acted that way when he was stoned. I used to hang out a lot at Bob and Fran's, and we became good friends. Fran and I sometimes cleaned her house together while we were high on Benny's. Many of the bikers and hippies hung out at their house, too. They would really talk with a lot of profanity. I didn't like it, especially the "f" word. I made a deal with them. I said, "I'd really appreciate it if you didn't talk that way when you're in my house." They honored that. If I was up in Bill's shop, and they started cussing, I didn't say anything. When they came to the house though, they'd make a point not to use the "f" word. The hippies honored me with this, too. It was pretty amazing actually.

-Chapter Eighteen-

Broken Hearted and Alone

Bill and I began going up to Portland to see the bikers, to hang out, to have parties, and to buy bike parts. During that time, I learned the bikers' rules. First off, women are not worth anything. They can be traded for a pack of cigarettes, a can of beer, joints, anything. If a girl got on the back of a motorcycle with a biker, she is giving him permission to do whatever he wants with her. Sex was very loose among the bikers.

Another rule is that the bikes are the first priority. The guys went through initiations, which involved sexual acts. It all was very perverted even to the extent of using a woman, who was called a biker's mama. She had to be emotionally destroyed so that she would be willing to do anything and everything with all the men. It was strange, even with all the disrespect to women and competition among the men, how there was an intense brotherhood among the bikers. Bikers accepted one another, had nicknames for one another, and had a strict and organized code to keep order in the community. They had a president, vice- president, secretary, and a clubhouse. As long as a biker was a member of the gang, he could crash at the clubhouse anytime he wanted. It was like a home.

This particular chapter of the gang was not really violent even if they were a chapter of the "Hell's Angels." They would rip something up or burn something down, but to my knowledge, they never murdered anybody outright. If someone died in a fire they started, they never considered it murder, even though it was.

They did stick up for one another. If one biker ripped off another, they would go after the one who stole from the other. If it was a woman who stole from them, God help her. They had an unwritten code that had to be obeyed. The code was centered on the belief of "One for all, and all for one." There is a lesson to be learned from that devotion to one another. My mother later wrote a song about it.

The guys had respect, for the most part, for each other, but the bikes were the main things. They would go on bike runs for two or three days to a particular place to party for two or three more days. Anything goes at those parties. Drugs were big. Bill still went to his shop by his mom's house to work on old cars. He also worked on models at the house at a desk that he set up in our basement apartment. Meanwhile, I stayed involved with crocheting and working.

We visited different people all the time. There was a man and his wife with two boys who were into racing, and we visited them. They knew a lot about cars. We'd go there about 10:00 in the morning and stay until 9:00 at night. Bill would visit with the guys, and I'd stay in the house. She would just feed us all, which was a God send because we didn't have a lot of food. She was a really cool person, fun to be around, and down to earth; I really enjoyed when we visited them.

I would ask Bill a lot of questions about how he knew certain people. I got yelled at for that because I wasn't supposed to ask a lot of questions. The police often showed up to the apartment next door to us because there was a lot of drug trafficking there. One night, Bill and I were awakened in the middle of the night by the banging and bumping around in the upstairs apartment. The man upstairs had taken acid and thought he could fly, so he jumped out the window. We found out later that the man died of an overdose and from the fall from the third floor window.

Bill decided that he was going to make another pair of slicks from a new pair of black jeans, so he went and bought them. We really did not have the funds at the time. The bikers never washed their slicks because the more dirt and grease you got on them, the slicker they became, and water would just run off of them. The slicks were great for riding bikes, but they also got everything that you sat on filthy. When I saw Bill making slicks like I had noticed before, I secretly took a pair of pliers and ripped the teeth out of the zipper one at a time, so that his zipper would break, and he'd have to start all over again. I was ornery and hard to get along with at the time.

Another time Bill was making a pair of slicks out of new black jeans. I gathered up the clothes, including his new slicks, to take them to the laundromat, and when I came home, he was so angry that he flung me all over the cement floor because I had washed the pants that he was making slicks out of. I went to the kitchen and got a knife and told him that if he was going to treat me like that, to just kill me. He broke the knife and began throwing me head first on the cement floor. He finally left, but came back later with a fake leather skirt and vest to give me for Valentine's Day, and he apologized to me. The next week, I packed up my stuff and left. I stayed with my aunt and uncle for quite a while and found a job at a nursing home. Bill lost the basement apartment because he never paid the rent.

I know Bill had stolen a lot of stuff, even from people that he knew and even from people who had been good to us. I had told him, "What goes around, comes around, and God didn't like what he was doing." When I left Bill, he lost the apartment, his job, and his bike and the car shop burned to the ground all in one week. Most of his car parts got stolen from him, and he didn't have anything left. I felt sorry for him, so I found him and went back to live with him. He admitted to stealing and treating me badly. Bill had a paneled truck that he parked in the carport at his mom and dad's house. I made a bed in the back of the paneled truck that was in the carport and that was where we lived. We ate out of his parents' house and kept going to parties.

Bill went up to Portland for a party, and I drove the paneled truck up after I got off of work. I took Jackie, whom I just met, and some other young men and women I did not know with me because Bill had told me to. When we arrived at the clubhouse, I met a heavy set woman who had two kids. The boy was about two years old and had a kitchen towel wrapped around his bottom, which was so wet and filled with waste that it was all running down his legs. The three year old girl had a flimsy dress on and wet pants, too. I took the boy and cleaned him up. I went in where the biker chicks were and found something I could use for a diaper and wrapped him up. Jackie helped me clean up the girl. The woman had no clothes for the kids and was doing something with the bikers, so I took the kids and bedded them down in the panel truck. I didn't think about putting plastic on, so they urinated all over the mattress. I waited for Bill to come out to the panel, but he never did. So I went into the biker's clubhouse and started to go into the bedroom. I heard a gun click, and I couldn't get in the room. The door finally opened, and I went up to Bill in the top bunk and asked him what he was doing. I saw the heavy set woman on the table and realized that she was a biker's mama. A biker's mama is a woman that is emotionally destroyed to the point that she must have sex because it is the only source of love and acceptance to her. I stayed with Bill for a while, and then I decided to go back to the truck. After the bedroom door was opened, I assumed the woman had slept with Bill. I found out later that this was part of the motorcycle gang's initiation. The gang initiation required that you sleep with the biker's mama with a witness watching you while the girlfriend or wife is at the party. The gun click that I had heard was the witness that was protecting Bill and the biker's mama's actions.

The next morning, I got up and Jackie got into the panel truck with me. Jackie, the kids, and I spent the night in the panel truck. Bill told me that he was going to take this biker mama back on the bike so she'd have a ride home. He took off on the motorcycle with her. I took the kids in the back of the panel truck. I floored it trying to catch up with them. They stopped at a gas station, and they were laughing about making a fool out of me. I had a primary chain wrapped around my waist as a belt. I passed them at the gas station. I stopped the panel truck and waited. When they flew down the road on the motorcycle past me, I took off the primary chain belt and swung it at them. I missed them by about an inch. I had it in mind to kill both of them. I thank God that I didn't. I have never been as angry as I was that day.

We all got back to Dad and Mom Pearcy's home. Bill and the other woman got there before me, and I pulled in with the kids in the back. I have no idea how I didn't blow up the engine. Bill got off the bike and came over to say something to me. I just cursed him out. The girl got off the bike and said that Bill was going to help her move. I said, "No he's not. You're going to come with me right now, and I'm going to move you!" She got in the car with me and her kids. We went to the biker mama's house to help her pack. I was so mad that I packed her up in record time. I noticed some of my clothes and jewelry at her house and some of Bill's clothes, too. I finally connected the dots and realized where I was getting genital crabs from. I had to burn the sleeping bag in the truck once because of the crabs that Bill brought home. Bill was not impressed that I was burning the sleeping bag, and I thought he was going to beat me up. I am pretty sure he was thinking this was not a good time to push me. Every time I got a box packed, I'd shove it at her in her large heavy set chest as hard as I could. It had to have hurt her, but she never flinched.

I don't know where she stayed that night, but I went and got my dog and went to Bob and Fran's house. The next morning, I went to the welfare office to report the woman and the way she treated her kids. I gave the social worker every detail I could, and Jackie was with me as a witness. Believe it or not, as I was talking to the social worker, the biker mama came in with both kids dressed in their Sunday best and each one holding a Bible. The social worker took the biker mama's word over mine and Jackie's. I couldn't believe it. She picked up her food stamps and welfare check. Bill came and went for about four months. I was like a now and then wife. It was very hard not knowing where he had been, what he had done, or who he was with. During those months, I went and visited Bob, Fran, and my new friend Boots a lot. Boots was a biker's wife who had six children, and I used to hang out with her. I don't think I had a phone because I couldn't afford one. I began working at two nursing homes from 7:00 PM until noon the next day and was trying to make money to live.

During all of this instability, my dog, Sheba, got hit by a car. I didn't think that she was going to make it, and I had no money to take her to a vet. A woman that I didn't even know stopped to help me after the car that had hit Sheba kept going. She picked up Sheba and took us both to the vet to have the dog worked on. I kept crying because I didn't have any money, and I was afraid Sheba was going to die. The woman took Sheba to her vet, and she took me home while the dog stayed. The dog was in the hospital for five days.

The woman went with me to pick her up. I told the vet that I didn't have the money, but I would pay it even if I had to get another job. I brought Sheba home, and the woman paid for the medicine for Sheba and got her a new bed. When I went back to make the first payment to the vet, I was told that the bill had already been paid in full by the woman. Sheba came out of it eventually. I was so thankful to this lady, but I had no idea where she lived so that I could send her a thank you note. She did come and visit Sheba once to see how the dog was, and I thanked her then.

I became close to Boot's children who hung around my house. Boot's husband had left them, and I was like a second mother to them. I met some new friends, Danny and Jerri, at Bob and Fran's house. Danny was a fun drunk, and when he got drunk or high, we could talk him into stuff. One night Danny, Bob, Fran, and I took Danny to a pizza restaurant, and we all got drunk. Fran and I convinced Danny that he owed us a steak dinner. Danny ended up sleeping it off at Bob and Fran's. The next morning we told him that he lost a bet the night before and owed us a steak and egg breakfast. We got it. It was fun cooking up schemes with Danny. We usually would tell Danny the truth after we had the dinner or breakfast.

Bill came and went. We fought all the time when he was home. He came back one time and stayed for about a week. I told him that, "Since we aren't getting along, and I have no idea where you've been these last four months, what I'd like to do is have you pack me up and take me back to Montana. That way I can go to school, get a data processing degree, and come back to support us. Then you can do whatever you have to do and I'll support you the rest of my life."

I was so down trodden. He laughed, but I didn't think it was funny. I didn't know what else to do. I didn't believe that divorce was right and since I had "made my bed, I had to lie in it," as the saying goes. I saw no way out. I now realize that Bill laughed because he was already dating Darla. Life was one big game to Bill. We were married when we were eighteen. Bill never took responsibility for anything. He grew up in a home where his mom wouldn't even claim him, and his dad was an alcoholic. There was constant fighting in his home. I can't imagine how he made it through school or anything else.

Bill stuck around for a few more days while I made arrangements to move back to Montana and go to school. I packed up what I had in the back of the car. I gave away the furniture that I had acquired from various places. Bill took me from Salem, Oregon back to Montana. Bill acted as if this was the end of our relationship. Bill told me that I never acted like a wife to him, but more like a mother. That hurt deeply, and I blamed myself for everything. I do not know how I could have been more of a wife to him. Bill stayed overnight in Montana and then took off. I went to data processing school for nine months and got my data processing degree. I also began cleaning people's houses and offices with Mom.

I missed Bill, but I knew I had to make a life for myself. I tried and tried to figure out why Bill said he loved me and yet treated me so badly. Mom and Dad were very supportive of me going to classes. I never told Dad about Bill beating me up; I think Dad would have killed him. I also never mentioned the drugs. The whole time I was going to IBM school, I would pray almost every night that Bill or I would die so we would not get a divorce. There were times that I cried myself to sleep praying that prayer.

After I got the data processing degree, I went back to Salem and stayed with Bob and Fran. I finally tracked Bill down in Portland, and he was working as a mechanic on heavy machinery. Bill was always falling into these jobs that were a God send, although he never saw them that way. I did talk to him about God, but he just rejected the whole idea. It was as if he wanted to go to hell. When he saw me at his work, he didn't respond or anything. He told me that he was going to divorce me and marry another lady. I found some letters in his car and read them. He had been with her quite a while, and she was carrying his baby.

I tried to keep Bill and spent the night with him that night. I was so desperate that I told him that if I couldn't have him, I wanted to have his baby. He just laughed and said that a lot of women had told him the same thing. That night, he cooked himself a steak and just gave me a couple of bites to eat. He told me that I had gotten fat, and he was right.

I still hung around him and tried to get him back. Just before September, I found out that they were going on a motorcycle run. I told him that I wanted to go on that run, but he said that he was going to take Darla. I said, "You don't want to do that. If you go on this motorcycle run, you won't come back." He said, "Don't threaten me..." I said that I was not threatening him, but that I just knew. I talked then about God and about Bill needing to turn his life around. He said that he didn't want anything to do with God.

I left that afternoon very upset, knowing that I was going to get a divorce. I went back to Bob and Fran's. I was feeling very alone, stupid, disappointed, like a failure, unworthy, and grieved at the same time. I am sure I told Fran everything and probably got drunk that night, as if that would have solved anything.

-Chapter Nineteen-

Bill Pearcy's Death

I really loved Bill. I had fallen really hard for him. I do know that God protected me during that time. I could have gotten various venereal diseases, gotten hooked on drugs or alcohol, or suffered a lot of other consequences. I can hardly believe how protected I was.

It was mid September. Esther and Ben lived next door to Bob and Fran. That was a bad marriage, too. Ben treated Esther just horribly. I had woken up one night from a horrible dream about Bill getting hurt. I had felt a heaviness on my chest and just started crying. The next day a call came in at Esther's house. She came to Fran's house and got me. Mom Pearcy was on the phone and asked if I was alone or if someone was with me. I said, "Bill's dead, isn't he?" She said, "No, he was killed in a drowning accident." I said, "What's the difference?" I got off the phone, and I was just screaming. Fran told me later that I took a hold of her hands and just started screaming, "He's dead, he's dead, he's dead!"

When I was going to school, I remember praying quite a few times that God would either take me home or take him out so I wouldn't have to get a divorce. I repented of that prayer a long time ago. I was so stupid. Esther tried to talk to me, but I just left to go to Fran's. They finally got me settled down enough to find out what happened in Bill's drowning accident.

I knew that I needed to go to the Social Security Office to get the burial benefit. I found out that they wouldn't do anything without a body. I went to the Veterans' office for the two hundred fifty dollars to help me bury Bill. They wouldn't do anything either. I went to a funeral home to ask them some questions, but they wouldn't do anything without a death certificate. I went to the police department and was told that no death certificate could be issued until they found the body. The Idaho police department gave me details of what took place. The police department in Salem, Oregon was very little help because the accident happened in Emmett, Idaho. Apparently, Bill and the motorcycle gang had stolen a houseboat in Emmett, Idaho. About six of them were on the boat while Bill was working with his mechanical

To Hippies, Bikers, and Punks With Love

tools, which he carried in his leather jacket and in his pants. The carburetor caught on fire and exploded with some sharp metal hitting Bill in the chest. He died on September 5, 1971.

They told me that the chances of finding the body were slim. I finally called my mom and dad from Esther's. They came out to see me and to help me. My aunt and uncle came out also. The police were telling me that I could hold a fake funeral and then get a death certificate. I refused to have a fake funeral and then do a normal one later. God was kind, and the body was found fourteen days later.

I met with the Social Security officials, and I got the run around. The man asked me all kinds of questions. I had to have my marriage license, birth certificate, proof of who I was, etc. Then he asked me if our marriage had been consummated. I was angry and yelled a few choice words. He settled me down and issued the two hundred fifty-five dollars to me in my name and the funeral home's name and mailed it to the funeral home. I felt like the Social Security officer did not trust me and was accusing me of lying. But I was glad they finally gave me the money.

Mom helped me go to the bank to get his money out of the savings account. It was only about five dollars. They gave me a hard time there, too. I remember saying something like, "What would you do if this were five thousand dollars rather than five dollars?" They wanted all the papers, and Mom Pearcy had to sign the money over to me. Mom Pearcy wanted half of the money for all her trouble. I told her that if she wanted half of the five dollars, then she needed to help me with half of the bills. She hung her head and signed it over to me. The bank also helped me to get Bill's bike and car transferred over to me so I could sell them.

I had the bike brought over to Bob and Fran's house. My mom and dad stayed for the funeral. I had a biker funeral because that would have been what Bill wanted. Dessi, Bill's best friend, and some other officers came from Portland. They asked me what I wanted. I just wanted Bill to be taken to the grave site and have the services there. I told him that I would like to ride in the funeral procession with the bikers. Pogo, the president, told me that he would allow that, and he would give me a biker to ride with, and he'd leave me alone. He was going to do this in regard to Wild Bill, which was Bill's nickname in the motorcycle gang. They were very good. I was surprised at how the bikers treated me, but I am sure it was out of respect for Wild Bill. My mother wrote a song about the bikers:

"Bikers form a club to live in a pack; stories of their lives within

would fill a mighty rack. And when it comes to trouble inside

of the club, they'll form a solid golden band of brotherhood

and love. Give their all together to ease a single pain and when

it's all aborted, they're on the run again.

Run, boy, run, run for the sun.

The devil's goin' to catch ya, boy, no matter how you run."

Mom Pearcy had gotten a job being a companion to a lovely lady, Mrs. Johnson. Mom Pearcy told Mrs. Johnson that I was making her pay all of Bill's funeral and for his debts, and had asked Mrs. Johnson to help her with the money. Mrs. Johnson called my mother to check out the story. Mom was just livid. Mom got a hold of me, and we went to an appointment together to see Mrs. Johnson while Mom Pearcy was out of the house. Mrs. Johnson told us that she had been asked for five thousand dollars to pay for the funeral. I told Mrs. Johnson that I was going to pay for this and had not asked anybody for money. Mom backed me up and told her that I hadn't even let them help out with the finances for the funeral. Mrs. Johnson was very nice about the whole thing and said that she was suspicious and thanked us for our honesty. I was so angry and disappointed that Mom Pearcy could do such a thing. It seemed like a soap opera to me.

After getting money from the Veterans' Office and Social Security, I was short twenty-two hundred dollars for the funeral home expenses. I found someone who was interested in Bill's bike and offered him a deal of twenty-two hundred dollars for the bike. He gave me twelve-hundred dollars and wrote me a promissory note of five hundred dollars and a promissory note of five hundred dollars to the funeral home.

I stayed at Bob and Fran's for a while. I tried to get welfare, but couldn't because I had no children. I was able to get food stamps though. Pogo, Dessi, and Big Red came later to check on whether or not the promissory notes were even paid for. I told them no. Pogo had it taken care of. Later, I heard from other hippies that the biker who had bought Bill's bike had his shop burned down and that he and his old lady had some broken bones and were run out of town.

After the funeral, we had a party. I saw Darla there and she was pregnant with Bill's child. I talked to her. She said, "You know, Bill made you out to be really mean, but you're really nice." We talked about him extensively. Shortly after the funeral, I started writing letters to Darla all the time. Darla had lost the baby. Her mom wrote to me and asked me to stop writing because Darla felt guilty about what took place, so I stopped.

Mom also presented the song to the bikers at the wake. They were quite impressed with the song. Later on, I crocheted a giant hanging rug with a Sportster bike like Bill had. Grody, one of the bikers, went to the biker's club house with me so that I could present this to them to put in their club house. The president told me at that time that I had better not come back because I was no longer attached to anyone, and I would be open game. I thought that was pretty nice of him to tell me that because he didn't have to.

I stayed at Mom Pearcy's house while she was a companion to Mrs. Johnson. I filled out all of the papers for the Veterans' widow's pension. Eventually, I got eighty-seven dollars a month. I was a mess and stayed pretty much to myself for six to eight months. After that time of grieving, I was determined to get a job and went around the Portland area to find one. I finally got a data entry operator position at Oregon Pacific Industries. It was a small office and a good job. The other two ladies I worked with were really nice to me. We would go to lunch often together. It seemed strange to me. A housing development went up next to Mom Pearcy's house. They didn't want Mom Pearcy's house and Bill's old shop around their new development, so they began dumping trash in the yard. One night I noticed a bunch of nails in the driveway, and I just picked them up. The next night there were more nails and a friend of mine backed over them and got a couple of his new tires flattened. I was being accused of having wild parties and began getting a lot of crank phone calls. Some guy called me quite regularly and pretended to be Bill and said that he was still alive. I changed my number several times, and it just didn't do any good. The person sounded a lot like Bill too, which did not help my emotional state of mind. I talked to Bob and Fran a lot about these phone calls. Fran and I tried to figure out who was making them. Bob did some checking as well for me. Emotionally, I was such a mess. I went up to 185 pounds and realized that I needed to get it together.

There was another hippie named Sherry, who I met at Bob and Fran's house. She helped me lose a lot of weight, and I went down to 125 pounds in about one year's time. At 125 pounds, men became interested in me again. I probably would have been better off not losing the weight. I began to get pretty promiscuous. I started dating some real losers, including a married man who was dating several girls in order to borrow money from each of us. I did not know that Jerry was married at the time that I was dating him. Jerry finally told me that he was separated. Something did not add up. I made some phone calls to find his wife. She admitted to me that Jerry was dating two others besides me so he could get five hundred dollars from each of us so he and his wife could leave town. Needless to say, I was a pretty angry person anyway. So I gathered up Jerry's clothes that I had and went down to the car dealership where he worked. I made sure his underwear was on top of the stack. I entered his office at the car dealership at the busiest part of the day. In front of customers, I dumped his clothes out of the box and onto his desk. I told him off loudly and left.

I was on the verge of insanity and began to just hide in the house. God sent a really good friend to me. Larry came over and knocked on the door. I wouldn't answer, so he went to the windows and told me to answer the door. I let him in, and he insisted that we were going to the ocean and have a good time. I refused, but he kept insisting. So I gave in, and we went to the ocean. We had a fun time, and we went to a club. I'll never forget it. I won this really pretty clock in a raffle. I was emotionally uplifted because of that. Larry let me use him as a sounding board. He was just a really good friend. He'd bring his girlfriend out sometimes, and we'd just visit and spend time together.

Larry finally moved out of Salem, Oregon. Boots wanted to go to California, so she asked me if I'd watch the six kids and get them in school. The kids moved in with me into Mom Pearcy's house. Mom and Dad came in town and helped me deal with some things. Dad helped me ship all of Boots' stuff to her out in California. I had a lot to deal without having to deal with her stuff, too. Mom dealt with the neighbors, and they began to leave me alone. We had a party at the house and sang, "Mind Your Own Business" with the windows open. Dad helped me get rid of a guy who was insistent that I was the woman of his dreams. He had told his parents that we were going to be married. He kissed like a fish, and I didn't want anything to do with him. He wouldn't take no for an answer. This guy would call me, and I'd go take a shower, roll my hair, and come back, and he'd still be on the phone. When Dad came, he took care of the issue. I never knew what Dad told him, but I am sure it was really good.

I worked for two years at OPI Lumber Company and ended up working a job that was meant for three people. I asked for a raise but was turned down, so I gave my two week notice. I told Dad that I was moving back to Montana. It was time to pack it in and move on. During the last two years, I had been faced with many deaths, so many that a spirit of grief had settled in on me. God eventually delivered me from the grief, but it was difficult with so many deaths at one time.

Prior to Bill's death, Dad Pearcy died of a heart attack, and Nanna Pearcy died a couple of months before that. Mom had gone to Nebraska, and Grandma passed away. I was close to my grandma, and I did not have time or money to go visit her. I also lost my two dogs, Lady and Sheba. One year later after Bill Pearcy's death, on the exact date and time, Mom Pearcy died. Grandpa Pearcy died around that time, too. There were other relatives that passed away also. I never had time to deal with all the grief.

On March 15, 1973, my dad and his friend came to pick me up. I got rid of everything except what would fit in the pickup truck and my car. I left Oregon, and I went back to Helena, Montana. By that time, my friend Boots had gotten the kids and moved out to California. I got a job working for the highway department as a data entry operator with around ten girls working in the office. I was such a mess. I couldn't make friends. I felt like I never fit in and felt as if I couldn't do a good job. I really felt like I was not worthy of anyone's friendship. I thought I was boring to be around. I still deal with some of this today. Dad helped me make a plan to pay off all my bills and theirs. Mom and I worked together cleaning houses and offices, and it was a successful plan. In about a year and a half, we had paid off all our bills and the trailer, pickup, Mom's car, and my car. Before that, I had owed twenty-six hundred dollars in credit card debt. Dad then got a job in construction in Idaho, and Mom and Dad moved. I stayed in an apartment in Helena. When Mom and Dad were killed, I brought the trailer over to Clancy and set it up.

While I was in Clancy I tried to teach myself how to sew. I visited Russ, Terri, Bob, and Fran a lot. I tried not to visit these people a lot as I thought I would wear out my welcome and they would reject me eventually. Then I met Bill Zabel in a bar and our relationship flourished from there.

-Chapter Twenty-

Continuing in My Spiritual Walk

Now Will and I are together and living in Charlotte, North Carolina. I am still a work in progress. God has healed me of a great deal of sorrow and grief, anger and rage, bad feelings towards others, foul mouth abuse, and shameful utterances from my lips. I've taken correction from others. I've been as obedient to God as I possibly can be. Again, I'm still a work in progress. I am still working out things with my husband, Will.

We are pressing into God as much as we know how. We are working with one another. We are in a particular body of believers for this time. I was in the women's ministry for a while. There has been a great deal of healing there. A lot of my mind sets from the past and attitudes of the past were changed when I served in the woman's ministry as a prayer warrior. As a result of the women's ministry, there is a group of four ladies that I still pray with. God has put a unity among us that is unbelievable.

The enemy has tried to put a stop to the diligent prayers, but we are standing our ground. I still have a hard time believing that anyone would want to be friends with me, but I believe God is working on that, too.

Out of the loneliness, rejection, guilt, shame, and a whole lot of fear, the Lord has risen up a determined, faithful prayer warrior who now knows that she is not alone. What the enemy had meant for evil, God is turning around for good before my very eyes. I am still going from glory to glory. Just last week, I was asking God about all of the correction that I was getting from other people in the body of Christ. I was getting upset all week about the correction, and I knew there was a spiritual problem causing my frustration. I asked God about the correction and forgot about it.

One day while I was calmly sewing a shirt, the Lord brought to my remembrance that my dad had always yelled at me when I did something wrong and never praised me when I did something right. The Lord told me that a root of rejection had formed, and I never felt as if I could measure up. I forgave Dad for making me feel unworthy and rejecting me in that way. I forgave myself for receiving the rejection and unworthiness.

The Lord also revealed that Will needed to pray against his sense of rejection and unworthiness. We prayed together and were healed. On the following Sunday during worship, the Lord reminded me that He set me free first so I could be used by Him to deliver others. The Lord told me to share this spiritual freedom with a group leader who was at a deliverance retreat. I did so, and he was delighted. In writing this book, I realized that I needed to issue forgiveness to some people. I was able to do so with the help of the Holy Spirit and have been set free because of it.

In a home group at my church, people began asking me if I was a Native American because my prayer language sounded like a Native American language. I was asked this question so much that I began to ask God what was the dialect of my prayer language. I felt like God wasn't going to answer me, so I stopped asking. It was close to summer when Will and I decided to go backpacking on the Appalachian Trail starting in Massachusetts. We had to leave the trail because I had something going on with my right leg. We got the car and drove to Maine. We stayed overnight at Mt. Katahdin. I noticed early the next morning as we were feeding the chipmunk and having breakfast, that there was a certain peace in the area. It was like I was home. There was an excitement in the air for me. We drove to the trail head and started hiking up this tough mountain. The more we hiked, the more I felt this peace and spiritual connection. I didn't say anything to Will. I didn't want him to think I was crazy. After about four miles of hiking, Will said that I was too tired, and we needed to turn around. The hike up was pretty tough. Will let me sit down, and he went further up to take some pictures since we were required to hike up and down the mountain in one day. I was still feeling the amazing peace. We got a hotel room for the night. I finally told Will how I was feeling and how I sensed it was God. Will told me that he was feeling that peace too, and he wanted to take me to some places to visit.

I told Will about praying about my prayer language, and he got excited. So we went to the Penobscot Native American information center. We watched a movie there, and as I watched that movie, I heard my prayer language. It was a spiritual experience for me. I learned from the movie that Mt. Katahdin was where the Native Americans did their spiritual practices. Many of their beliefs lined up with the Word of God and godly principles such as unity, giving, brotherly love and taking care of their elderly, widows, and children that are alone. There were a lot of articles that the Native Americans had made that I liked, some I even had at home. I began to share with Will what I was experiencing in my spirit. He felt as if I was right on target, so we went to some more shops around there. Some of the designs that represented God, like beaded earrings, were just like we made at home. It amazed me that the items were the same as those I had at home. Prior to this time, I never knew the Penobscot Native Americans ever existed. God spoke to my heart that day and told me that my prayer language was that of the Penobscot Native American. I could hardly wait to get back to my home group to let them know.

Now God is working with me to work with other people and to love other people like He loves them. He's teaching me how to minister to other people. It is a scary thing for me, and at the same time, it's very rewarding and absolutely who I am in God. One time, we were in a women's conference with the women's ministry, and I was used in the capacity of laying hands on others. I saw many ladies receive from the Lord, and I am in awe that God would use me in this manner, and it is very fulfilling to me.

While meeting with my prayer group one day, I found out that some people were laughing because I was attempting to write a book. One Monday morning in prayer, other prayer warriors also felt as if others were laughing about this book because my English and writing are so horrible. God is the God of the impossible. He has us do what is impossible for us to do. For me to write this book by myself is impossible, but with the help of a very dear prayer warrior, we wrote this book together in God. It is my prayer that each and every person that reads this book is totally freed from any addictions, any lies that the enemy tells us in our mind, and that you have full understanding that Jesus loves you!

-Chapter Twenty-One-

Take God Out of the Box

The word "deliverance" is defined in the Webster Dictionary as a "setting free, rescue, or release." My idea of deliverance is a trust in God and believing that God can do anything for you and can set you free in your mind, will, and emotions. All things are possible with God. Anything that someone sets their mind to, they can have by faith. On God's golden altar, we lay our fleshly desires down and let God have His way, trusting that His way is the best way for us. It is a willingness to release ourselves to God to change the things in our lives that we know or don't yet know is sin. There are several ways in which I can recall my deliverance experiences occurring with God's divine intervention.

Will and I had gone to several meetings and teachings on the use of prayer cloths as taught out of the Word of God. Will and I both picked up a prayer cloth at a conference. At that time, I was suffering from severe bronchitis two or three times a year. I wore that prayer cloth pinned under my clothes until it was just shredded. Will and I believed that the bronchitis would be destroyed because sickness and disease does not belong to me. Will and I were diligent to pray daily in agreement against the main causes of the bronchitis. There was an emotional root of self-pity that needed to be destroyed. Every year, the effects of the bronchitis lessened until it left for good. I still have some symptoms from time to time, but I immediately proclaim that it has no right to me, and the symptoms disappear within minutes.

Deliverance occurs when you pray for revelation knowledge before you read the Word from the Bible. I used to spend hours in the Word after I had asked for revelation knowledge. I prayed in the Spirit and read the Word at the same time. I was told that I couldn't do that, and it wouldn't work, but I did. It causes revelation knowledge of the Word because God shows up.

During praise and worship, there have been countless times of deliverances in my personal experience. Our pastor would sometimes lead us into singing in tongues, and we sensed that the congregation was floating into the throne

To Hippies, Bikers, and Punks With Love

room of God. It was real awesome to be in the presence of God. We'd be so caught up with being with God, and then it would get really quiet. We were like Mary sitting at the feet of Jesus. We'd come out of those services, being set free, and we didn't even know what happened.

There have been times where I'd be all bent out of shape when I went to a Sunday service, and as I began to praise and worship God, I'd begin to be so filled with peace and settle down that I'd forget what I was fussing about. I've also had the Holy Spirit say to me that I had wrong thinking patterns. I was directed by the Holy Spirit to change the way I was thinking about someone or about a certain incident.

I've had the Holy Spirit give me words for three or four people at the same time. I had to ask Him what order He wanted me to give them to the people. Being put out under the power of the Lord and letting the Holy Spirit minister to you is a remarkable form of deliverance. There were probably five or six times that I was put out under the power of the Lord, and the Holy Spirit ministered to me in several ways concerning the rape incident in my life. The Holy Spirit led me into forgiving others when I couldn't do it on my own. He even had me pray for those who raped me. Even if it was hard on my mind, emotions, and my will, the obedience to God was necessary and well worth it. I remember that every time I got off the cold cement floor, some anger would leave, I could feel the peace of God, and I would act differently afterwards. When you feel like you are a prisoner in your mind, your emotions, and in your will, it is a horrible way to live. But there is nothing like the feeling when you know that those bars are totally melted, and you've been totally changed.

Deliverance is about a willingness to forgive. When someone tells you something that affects you and causes you to react, you need to ask God why you have that certain reaction. Keep still about it and pray. So many times, believers in Jesus will be around other believers and fuss and get offended. When another believer hurts your feelings, they didn't get up that morning and decide to hurt your feelings. You are responding to those feelings because of something you received from the enemy in the past. That's the way it operated in my life. When I would meet someone new, I would assume that I would make a mistake in front of them and they would not like me. That was not reality. My first pastor and his wife were absolutely wonderful when it came to this matter. They said, "Keep it to yourself, keep still about it, start praying about it, and start asking God if it is something to do with you." I found out that 99.9% of the time there was some issue with me; not the other person. This is a way to put a stop to a lot of the strife that is in church today.

Listening to preaching and teaching of the Word is absolutely imperative. Faith comes by hearing, and hearing by the Word of God (Romans 10:17). I would listen to teaching tapes by my pastor, and other men and women of God over and over and over again. Sometimes I'd have someone record it for me. It causes faith to grow. You get so much of the living Word on the inside of you, and your spirit is already alive that it gives life to your bones, emotions, and mind. You receive it by an act of your will. Whatever God points out to you, you need to issue forgiveness and change. Always ask the Holy Spirit to show you how you're different. It will encourage you for the next time.

John 14:16 says, "And I will ask the Father and He will give you another comforter (counselor, helper, intercessor, advocate, strengthener, and standby), that He may remain with you forever." The Holy Spirit is my best friend. He will be there to tell you what you need when you need it if you will trust and rely on Him (Proverbs 3:4-6).

There have been countless times in my prayer closet where I've just sat at Jesus' feet to listen. Sometimes I just meditate on one scripture. In prayer, God will reveal things to you. I've asked for spiritual ears to hear His corrections. He is always faithful. Many times I've had our first pastor look at me, stop in the middle of his sermon, and give a prophetic word to me or someone else in the church. If you don't want everything God's got for you, if you only want a portion of it, He'll give you that portion. But I'm telling you, you're missing out if you don't go with a spiritual hunger to get everything with tenacity and boldness. God loves boldness and loves when you press in. Because He loves me, that is what I decided to do.

When you pray with a group of people, especially with someone who is older in the Lord, deliverance can take place. Oftentimes, God will form a group of people who are so very different to pray together. I have sat in a prayer group with people who have completely opposite personalities, and we've just prayed in the Spirit. If all the people in the group are willing to do this and give up their pride, and just let God be Lord of their lives, change will occur. There is plenty to pray for: your pastor, your leadership, the town you live in, your boyfriend or girlfriend or spouse, or the neighborhood that you live in. Something happens when you're in corporate prayer. A godly unity shows up because of the love of God, and the differences in the group become precious to each one within the group. Of course, each person must be willing to change and to be open to God changing them and give up their ideas and opinions if you want godly unity.

Fellowship is a blessing. Go out to lunch or have coffee with someone. Make a point to get together with other people to talk. Make up your mind to care about others and get your mind off yourself. Ask others about their families and lives. The whole time that they share with you, they will deposit their anointing from the Lord into your life. Have the courtesy and patience to sit and listen to them. I had to learn to do this. It was totally against my nature. I was never taught to say "please" or "thank you." I've learned to be excited about other people's lives, and I tell you, it is a blessing. Start focusing on the other person and ask them questions about their lives. You'll not only bless people this way, but you often have an opportunity to pray for them. When God has you pray for another individual and the struggles that they have, somewhere in the midst of it, God will set you free, often of the same type of struggle that they are having. As I have cleaned toilets, and I've cleaned for fifty plus years, there are times that God has shown me the grunge and dirt in people's lives. I pray as I clean, and the Lord gives me revelation knowledge of what needs to be prayed out of an individual's life. Sometimes He gives me a word or He relates it to something that I am cleaning, and I pray for their deliverance.

God has told me to intercede for someone and has sometimes even given them a prophetic word. There have been countless times that I was giving prophetic word to someone and was getting emotional healing for myself because God works in multiples. By the word "multiples," I mean that God will do more than one thing at a time by delivering the messenger giving the word and the person that is receiving the Word of the Lord. Deliverance can simply happen when you are just being quiet and listening to the Lord. Sometimes I've just wept in my chair and didn't know why, but then I would get a release from past hurts, just because of His sweet presence.

Testimonies are also a wonderful form of deliverance. They are important to hear and are greatly encouraging.

These programs, like "Cleansing Streams," use the Word of God and godly strategies to guide one gently through deliverance. Cleansing Streams teaches repentance, renouncing, breaking, and blessing. I like using the word "destroying" instead of "breaking" when you're talking about strongholds, but that is just a word preference that works for me. This program also has others pray for you at the deliverance retreat.

Someone has often come over to me in a church setting or at a home group to share a prophetic word and pray for me. It has really ministered to me. Sometimes it has been over the phone. Always be ready to receive. Often times, someone has called me on the phone on my busiest days. It was always wise to stop and listen to what the Lord my God had for me.

Forgiveness is so important in order to allow deliverance not only for you, but to release another person to be delivered. Forgiveness is commanded by God. Forgiveness is an act of the will. Often times, God helps you forgive as you begin praying for a person that has offended you. There was a particular lady that was mean to me. The Lord instructed me not only to pray for her, but I cleaned for her, gave her time, went to lunch with her, helped her move, and gave her gifts. God would specifically tell me what to give her. I have given offerings on her behalf and claimed it as seed for her deliverance. This has happened several times throughout my spiritual walk. This was done only through the guidance of the Holy Spirit. I know that some deliverance took place because I saw her actions change. While I was in Pennsylvania and attended a small group, two ladies were instructed by the Holy Spirit to shower me with gifts. These gifts were gifts of love, and I received them as gifts of love from God. As a result, gentleness began to replace the hard wall that I had formed around myself. I believe that this was instrumental in my deliverance from smoking.

If there is a particular song that ministers to you, by all means, listen to it as often as possible. It is amazing how music can minister to you. Lies of pride, shame, fear, etc. have been exposed as I've listened and sung along with some of my favorite music. Worshipping God is spiritual warfare, and we need to see it as such. God has been faithful to change me on a day to day basis. My last deliverance was with people praying for me using the Cleansing Streams method. The key to deliverance is to receive from God. Deliverance is an act of your will. God doesn't deliver you if you don't allow it because He will not override your will. I made up my mind that I wanted God to change me. I was and still am desperate for change in my life.

God can set you free whatever way He wants to, when He wants to, where He wants to, and how He wants to. You must be open for Him to change you. If you fight it, it will take longer and may not happen. Lie on that operating table and tell God that you are going to stay on it until He fixes you. Now I know that when I get in a particularly grumpy mood, I need some kind of deliverance. I get on that operating table as quickly as possible for my deliverance. Keep in mind, repentance always brings blessings. The Holy Spirit is a gentleman, and He will not force you to have deliverance in your life. One of my sister's in Christ said to me that the operating table is like the golden altar of God. There we can lay our flesh down and walk in the Spirit. I pray that I never forget that image. All of these deliverances I've gotten in my life have been rewarding and fulfilling experiences in the Lord. I am a better human being now than I ever was at thirty-six years old when this process started. Now I like myself. I pray that I always press into God and pray that you will too. I pray that you will press into the Lord and let Him set you free so that you have greater opportunities than I have had in the Lord.

To Hippies, Bikers, and Punks With Love

Made in the USA